50
CARD GAMES
for
CHILDREN

By
VERNON QUINN

With an Easy Lesson
in Contract Bridge
and
COMPLETE LAYOUTS FOR
PLAYI

THE UNITED STATE
CINCINNATI, OHIO   45212   U.S.A.

Copyright, ©*1956*
WESTERN PUBLISHING COMPANY, INC.

Racine, Wisconsin

PRINTING THIS EDITION 1983

To

Joan and Ann

and

Richard and Evan

of the House of Horace Miller

CONTENTS

CONTENTS—Continued

SOMETHING ABOUT CARDS

♣ SO long ago that no one knows how many hundreds or thousands of years, someone played the first game of cards.

The cards were not the neat oblong bits of pasteboard that we know, of course, but pieces of whatever material was at hand. Perhaps it was the cavemen who first thought of the game, playing it with leaves on which pictures of birds and flowers were scratched with sharp-pointed thorns.

The Chinese claim that they have been playing cards for thousands of years, and that their ancient sailors carried the game to India and other parts of Asia and to North Africa.

When the Crusaders—from France, Germany, England, Italy—marched upon Jerusalem in 1099, they found that one of the absorbing pastimes of the Saracens was playing cards. So perhaps it was the returning Crusaders who carried the game into the many countries of Europe from which they had come.

A few centuries later Cortes marched upon Montezuma's golden capital, Mexico, and the Spanish Conquistadores sat about camp playing cards—to the amazed interest of the Aztecs. That is the first record of playing-cards in America; but no doubt the men with Columbus, too, brought cards to while away the long ocean voyage.

In the early days playing-cards were often square

in shape; sometimes they were round; sometimes long and narrow.

And in those long-ago days the familiar Hearts, Clubs, Spades and Diamonds were not in use. Many different symbols were used; each country had its own. It would seem strange and amusing now to ask for "the 9 of Elephants" or "the 10 of Hawks"; yet these and other animals and birds were then common on playing-cards. Other symbols used were Leaves, Flowers, Bells, Acorns, Swords, Horsemen.

Playing-cards were not always intended for mere pastime, either. A teacher in England found his pupils very slow in learning grammar. He wrote the rules on a pack of playing-cards and, as a game, grammar was learned in no time! Soon packs of grammar-cards were being manufactured. And a little later a fascinating game of geography could be played with cards. Still other cards taught history.

When America began to manufacture her own playing-cards, she decided that she would have nothing to do with Kings and Queens. The patriotic New York manufacturer used the picture of George Washington for the "President of Hearts"; John Adams replaced the King of Diamonds; and Franklin and Lafayette headed Clubs and Spades. Instead of the four Queens, the goddesses of Love, Wisdom, Fortune and Harvests were used; and four Indian chiefs replaced the Knaves.

But the English cards were already so popular, in so many thousands of American homes, that the American cards never became well known. And today we have the Kings and Queens and Knaves—the fifty-two-card pack that is used in Anglo-Saxon countries the world over.

Wherever cards are played—in America, Europe, Asia, Africa, Australia—there are games that are similar. And most of the card games of today are based on games that have been popular for hundreds of years.

This book contains many of the old, old games which are still being played, and it has also some newer games, for an effort has been made to give *variety*—games for every occasion and every child.

Scores of children were consulted as to the games they play with their young friends or their parents, and only games that actually *are* played by boys and girls today (proving that they do understand them and enjoy them) have been included.

Thus it is truly a book of "Card Games for Children."

CARD GAMES THAT ARE FUN
TO PLAY

1. Menagerie

This is the jolliest of all party games—if nobody objects to noise!

Any number may play—the more there are, the more fun it will be.

First, everyone takes the name of an animal. The longer the name, the better the chance for winning. ("Hippopotamus—hippopotamus—hippopotamus!" is a fine tongue-twister!)

When everyone knows everybody else's animal-name, deal the fifty-two cards around, two at a time. (If some players have one more card than others, it does not matter.) Each player, without looking at his cards, stacks them face-down in a pile in front of him. The play is always in turn to the left.

The object is to win all the cards.

John, on the dealer's left, begins by taking the top card off his pile and flipping it over, face-up, on the table in front of his own stack. He is Rhinoceros, say, and he turns up a *Six*.

Mary (Buffalo), on his left, now quickly flips her top card face-up on the table in front of her; it is a *King*.

Bob (Kangaroo) turns over his top card. It is a *Six*—it matches John's card. Quickly John cries Bob's name three times, "Kangaroo—kangaroo—kangaroo!" while Bob is crying John's name, "Rhinoceros—rhinoceros—rhinoceros!" Whichever finishes the other's name first wins *all* the face-up cards of the other (in the first round there is only one, but later there are many). The one who wins puts the cards he receives *face-down at the bottom of his own face-down pile*.

Nancy (Giraffe), on Bob's left, turns her top card, perhaps a *Five*.

Then Tom (Chimpanzee) turns a *King*. If Mary cries, "Chimpanzee—chimpanzee—chimpanzee!" before Tom sees he has matched her card and calls the easier "Buffalo—buffalo—buffalo!" she wins his face-up pile, and puts it, face down, beneath her own face-down pile.

The play goes on, always in turn. Each upturned card is placed on top of the face-up stack, with only the top card showing. And every time anyone turns up a card that matches the top card of any pile, he and the player whose card he matches race to call each other's animal-name three times.

When a player's face-down pile is exhausted, he turns his face-up pile over, and begins to go through it as at the beginning, flipping the top card over when his turn comes.

If anybody calls a name in error, such as "Alligator —alligator—alligator!" when his card does not match any on the table, his face-up pile must be given to the one whose name he called.

When a player has no more cards, he is out of the game, and the others continue. Finally only two players are left. Then one of them gets all the cards, and wins the game.

♠ ◆ ♥ ♣

Another form of Menagerie that is great fun, is for each player to be a domestic animal or fowl, and not the *name* of the animal, but the *noise* it makes, must be called three times: such as "Moo—moo—moo!" "Meow—meow—meow!" "Quack—quack—quack!" "Gobble—gobble—gobble!"

2. Donkey

Donkey is a lively, noisy game for any number of players. Five or six make the best game.

First, place in the center of the table one less button (or bean, or anything for counters) than there are players—five buttons if there are six players.

The object is *not* to be the Donkey, but to be sure of grabbing one of the buttons when the time comes for the scrimmage.

A "set" of four cards means four of one denomination, such as four Aces, four Jacks, four Fives. Use as many "sets" as there are players. If there are six players, pick out six sets (any six) and put aside the remainder of the pack.

Shuffle the six sets thoroughly, and deal them

around, one card at a time, face-down. Each player will have four assorted cards. He picks them up and holds them fan-shape in his hand. He wants to get rid of his odd cards and get, as soon as he can, a complete set—four of a kind.

The dealer now cries, "Go," and immediately everybody, including the dealer rapidly passes one of his cards to the player on his left. This passing keeps up continuously all around the table, and as rapidly as possible, until some player finds all his four cards alike, a set. He cries, "Donkey!"—and everybody at the table grabs for a button.

The player who does not get a button has the letter D (the first letter in DONKEY) marked against him.

The cards are then shuffled again—only as many sets as there are players—and played as before. If someone else misses the button this time, he also gets the letter D. And if the same luckless player who already has a D should again miss the button, he is given an O to place beside his D.

As soon as anyone gets the six letters, D O N K E Y, he is the Donkey at the table and must bray "Hee-haw!" three times for the amusement of the other players.

That ends the game, and the one with the least number of letters against him wins.

3. Spade the Gardener

Any number may try their luck—and their wits—at capturing the Gardener and all his friends.

Only the twenty highest cards are used—the Ace, King, Queen, Jack, and Ten of each suit. And these cards have special names. (If six or more play, use the

Nines and Eights also, and call the Nines cats, and the Eights canaries.)

In the Spade suit, the King is *Spade the Gardener;* the Queen, *Spade the Gardener's wife;* Jack, *Spade the Gardener's son;* Ace, *Spade the Gardener's servant;* and the Ten, *Spade the Gardener's dog.*

In Diamonds, the King is *Sir Hinkam Funniduster;* the Queen, *Sir Hinkam Funniduster's wife;* Jack, *Sir Hinkham Funniduster's son;* Ace, *Sir Hinkam Funniduster's servant;* and Ten, *Sir Hinkam Funniduster's dog.*

In Hearts, the King is *Sir Hearty John,* and the Queen, Jack, Ace, and Ten are his wife, son, servant, and dog.

And in Clubs, the King is *Club the Constable,* and the Queen, Jack, Ace, and Ten are his wife, son, servant, and dog.

The object is for one player to capture all the cards.

Deal the cards around, one at a time.

Jerry, on the dealer's left, begins by asking anyone at all for any card. But he must be *very* sure to give its special name. He must say, "Dorothy, give me Club the Constable's dog" (and *not* "the Ten of Clubs"). Or, "Ann, give me Sir Hinkam Funniduster's servant" (never "the Ace of Diamonds"). If he makes a mistake in the name, he must give one of his cards to the player he asked (instead of getting a card himself), and the turn passes to her.

If Jerry asks correctly, however, and Dorothy has the card, she must give it to him. He then asks her, or any other player, for another card—being careful to give its special name. He continues as long as he gets the card he calls for.

When the player he asks does not have the card, it is then that player's turn. And he may begin, if he chooses, by asking John for all the cards, naming them one by one, that he knows John has just received.

He does not have to hold one card of a suit, to ask for that suit.

When a player has no more cards, he drops from the game, and the others continue. Finally one will hold all the cards, and he wins the game.

4. Snip-Snap-Snorem

Any number may play this lively old English game.

Deal out the full pack of fifty-two cards, two at a time. If some players have one more card than others, it does not matter. Each player picks up his cards and holds them fanshape, and the play is always in turn to the left.

The object is to get rid of your cards as quickly as possible.

John, on the dealer's left, lays any card at all on the table, face-up. The other players in turn either match it or pass.

Suppose John lays down a Nine. Mary, on his left, must put down a Nine, if she has one, and say, "Snip!" (If she has no Nine, she says, "Pass," and the first one on her left who has a Nine plays it and cries, "Snip!")

The next player who can, plays the third Nine, and cries, "Snap!" And the one who plays the fourth Nine cries, "Snorem!" and then has the privilege of beginning a new round. He lays down any card he pleases. And it in turn must be matched, the player of the second similar card crying, "Snip!"; the third, "Snap!";

and the fourth, "Snorem!" The lucky "Snorem" player always begins the next round.

If anyone, including the leader, has more than one of the cards led, he must play them all, one after the other (using the proper word with each card), and not hold one back for "Snorem."

The player who first gets rid of all his cards wins the game.

5. The Earl of Coventry

This is played like Snip-Snap-Snorem, except that instead of saying "Snip!" and "Snap!" and "Snorem!" *one line of a rhyme* is used by each player, beginning with the leader, and the fourth player *must* have the words "the Earl of Coventry" in this line. Each rhyme-line must be original, composed by the player of the card.

For instance, John leads a Six, and says, *"A little dog ran far away."*

Mary lays down the next Six, and says, *"He found a bone beneath some hay."*

Bob plays the third Six, with, *"He brought it home and gnawed all day."*

Betty, playing the fourth Six, adds, *" 'Twas the Earl of Coventry's old dog Tray."*

Then Betty, having played the fourth card, begins a new round, by leading any card at all; and she begins a new rhyme. She may mention the card in it, such as, *"Here's a fine Jack, all dressed in red,"* or, *"My play will be the Diamond Three."*

The player who begins the jingle should end his line with some word that is easy to rhyme.

The one who is first rid of all his cards wins.

This game is much more fun than Snip-Snap-Snorem, but it takes four times as long to play, for there are so many laughing-spells in between—every time a line is added to the rhyme! It really should be called the "Howling Game"!

6. I Doubt It

Any number may play—but they must keep their wits about them!

The object is to be the first to get rid of your cards.

Deal the cards around evenly, using the full deck. If one or two cards remain, lay them face-down in the middle of the table.

Each player takes up his cards and holds them fan-shape. The play is always to the left, in turn.

Billy, on the dealer's left, begins by laying on the table, *face-down*, from one to four cards, and saying, "It is one Ace" (or "They are two Aces," or whatever fits the number of cards he has laid down).

When Billy has laid down his cards, everyone, taking turns to the left, says either, "Pass," or, "I doubt it."

When someone says, "I doubt it," the cards Billy played are turned over. If they *are* two Aces (or whatever Billy has said) the one who doubts must take them up and add them to his hand. He must take, too, any others that are on the table. If they are *not* two Aces, and someone doubts it, Billy must take these cards, and any others on the table, back into his own hand.

If no one at all says, "I doubt it"—if everyone says, "Pass"—the cards are left face-down on the table, and the next one who must pick up cards adds these, too, to his hand.

Nancy, on Billy's left, has the next turn. She plays, face-down, any one to four cards she chooses, and says, "They are three Deuces" (or whatever fits); and everyone in turn says, "Pass," or, "I doubt it," as before. If someone doubts it and they are Deuces, he must add those and any other cards on the table to his hand. If they are not Deuces, Nancy must add them all to her hand. It is then the next player's turn.

The first player, when he puts down cards, must say they are *Aces;* the next player, *Deuces;* the third player, *Threes;* the next, *Fours;* and so on up to *Kings;* then begin again with *Aces.* A player must lay down at least one card when his turn comes whether he has a card of the proper value or not.

The first one to get rid of all his cards wins.

7. War

Very young players will like this simple game. It is especially good for those who know almost nothing about cards, for all they need to learn is the rank of the high cards—Ace, King, Queen, Jack, Ten.

War is a good game for two, or it may be played by three, four, or more.

The object is to win all the cards.

If two are playing, the pack is divided evenly, and each player, without looking at the cards, stacks them face-down in front of him.

Suppose Ellen and Mary are playing. Each plays the top card of her pile, laying it face-up on the table.

(Either one leads, or they play at the same time—it does not matter.) The one who has played the higher card—even if it is a different suit—takes both, and puts them, face-down, *at the bottom of her pile*.

Both play the next top card, and the higher wins.

And so on through the two piles.

If neither card is higher, but both alike (two Fives, two Kings) this brings on War. They are left on the table and Ellen and Mary each play another card, *face-down*, overlapping the first one; and another card, face-up, overlapping that; and the higher of the last two takes all six cards. If the last two should be alike, the War is Continued by each playing another face-down and face-up card and the winner takes all ten cards.

Soon one player will have lost all her pile of cards— and the other will have won the game.

(If three play, remove any one card from the pack. And have War whenever two cards are alike, such as two Fours and a Jack; and Double War if all three should be alike. If four or more play, decide at the beginning when there shall be War and when Double War.)

War

Continued War

Double War

8. Concentration

The player with the best memory, or with the ability to keep his mind from too much wool-gathering, will be the one to win this game. It is easy to play, and even the youngest children will find it fun.

Any number may play.

The full pack is used, and it may be *dealt* face-down on the table, in any number of rows, no two cards touching (this is the better way), or it may be merely spread face-down, the cards overlapping every-which-way.

The object is to win the greatest number of cards, by drawing pairs—two cards of the same denomination.

The play is always in turn to the left, and each player always draws *two* cards, one at a time.

David begins by drawing any two cards from the spread-out, face-down pack. He turns each of his two cards over as he draws it, so everyone can see what it is. If he has drawn a pair (two Fives, two Jacks, two Aces), he lays them beside him face-down, not to be used again in play, but to count for him toward game. He then draws two more cards, and continues as long as the two he draws form a pair.

If he draws two cards that do not match (such as an Eight and a King), after everyone has seen them *he returns them both,* one at a time, face-down, to the spread-out pack, placing them either back where he got them or anywhere else.

This is where the "concentration" comes in. Everybody watches closely to see just where David puts the King, and just where he puts the Eight; so when later someone draws a King for his first card, he will know precisely where to pick up a King for his second card, and so form a pair—two cards to count for him toward game. Or if someone draws an Eight he will know where to find another Eight.

Suppose David has put back a King and an Eight. It is next Judith's turn. She draws her first card and shows it. It is a Jack. She draws another card and shows it. It is a Ten. They do not match, so she puts them both back face-down, everyone watching to see where each card goes.

Now it is Carol's turn. She draws an Eight, and then, having a fine memory, she at once draws the Eight that David put back. Her two cards are a pair, so she lays them beside her, and she has another turn. She draws a Jack; she remembers where Judith put back a Jack, and draws it for her second card. Now she has another pair to add to her game-pile—and she has another turn.

She draws a King. She is sure she remembers where David put his King, but in the excitement she picks up the wrong card. It is a Seven; so she must put them both back, the King and the Seven, and the turn passes to the next player. If he has been alert, he can at once draw both David's King and Carol's.

And so the game goes on, each one continuing to play as long as he pairs two cards, and losing his turn and putting back two cards that do not match. Finally all the cards have been paired and laid aside.

Each player now counts the cards he has, and the one with the greatest number wins.

9. Rolling Stone

Perhaps this old German game was called Rolling Stone because the cards often roll back and forth, from one player to another.

Any number may play.

For four players only the thirty-two highest cards are used: A-K-Q-J-10-9-8-7 of each suit. (If five play, the Sixes and Fives are left in the pack. If six play, only the Deuces are removed. This will give each player eight cards.)

The object is to be the first to get rid of your cards.

Deal the cards around—three at a time, then two, then three. The player on the dealer's left then leads any card.

There are no trumps. Everyone must *follow suit* if he can. If everybody plays to the trick (each one being able to follow suit), the highest card wins. The trick is gathering in and laid aside face-down, not to be used again, and the one who wins it leads for the next trick.

When anyone cannot follow suit, he does not play some other card. Instead, he must pick up and add to his hand any card or cards already played on that trick. And he then leads *another suit*. (For example, if Richard leads a Spade, and Mary, next, has no Spade, she must pick up the card Richard played, add it to her hand, and lead some other suit. If Richard leads a Spade, Mary plays a Spade on it, Ellen plays a Spade, but Tom has no Spade, he must pick up the three cards played, add them to his hand, and lead another suit.)

The one who is first out of cards wins the game.

10. Linger Long

Four, five, or six players may see who can "linger longest" in this game.

The full pack is used. If there are four players, deal around, one at a time, until each player has nine cards; then place the remainder of the pack face-down in the center of the table. (If there are five players, deal eight cards to each; if six players, seven cards to each.)

The last card to the dealer is dealt face-up, and that suit is trump. Everyone picks up his cards and holds them fanshape.

The object is to take as many tricks as possible, so you will remain in the game to the end, for each time you take a trick you may add a card to your hand.

The player on the dealer's left leads. And all players, in turn, must *follow suit* if they can. If they cannot follow suit, they may play a trump, or any other card. The highest card of the suit led wins the trick, unless a trump has been played on the trick. (An Ace is higher than a King, but any trump is higher than the Ace of another suit.)

The winner of each trick lays the trick aside, draws the top card from the pack in the center of the table, adds it to his hand, and leads for the next trick.

As soon as a player is out of cards, he drops from the game, and the others continue to play.

The player who lingers to the end, still holding one or more cards when the others have none, wins.

11. Stay Away

Stay Away is based on an old French game. Instead of trying to take tricks, you try your very best *not* to take them!

While any number may play, it is best as a game for four, and it is more fun if the four players are not partners, but each fights for himself.

The object is not to win any trick containing a Jack, and so to have the lowest score when some player reaches 10. Nothing counts *for* you; and every Jack you win counts *against* you—the Jack of Spades 3 points, and each of the other Jacks 1 point.

Only the thirty-two highest cards are used, and they rank in the usual order: A-K-Q-J-10-9-8-7. (If there are five players, leave the Sixes and Fives in the pack —a total of forty cards. If six play, remove the four Deuces, and make the four Nines the unlucky cards to be avoided instead of the four Jacks.) Distribute the cards evenly—dealing three at a time, then two, then three.

There is no trump. The highest card of the suit led wins the trick. Everyone *must* follow suit if he can. Each time a player "revokes"—fails to follow suit when he can—he has 1 point marked against him.

Fred, on the dealer's left, leads. (He will want to lead a card lower than the Jack; otherwise he will be sure to catch a Jack on the first trick.)

The winner of each trick leads for the next one.

When all the cards have been played, the score is marked down—3 points for the one who has captured the Jack of Spades; 1 for the Jack of Hearts; 1 for the Jack of Diamonds; 1 for the Jack of Clubs. The thirty-two cards are then shuffled and dealt (by the next player on the left) for another round.

Points are not scored until the end of each round. When—at the end of a round, but not before—some player has 10 points against him, the game ends, and the one with the *least* number of points wins. If there is a tie, two players having the same low number, play one more round to settle it, adding the points of that round to the previous scores.

12. Hearts

This is an easy game for very young players. It may be played by any number, from two to six, but the best game is for four, playing separately or as partners. (If three play, remove one black Deuce from the pack; if five play, remove two black Deuces; if six, remove all four Deuces.)

The object is to *avoid* winning any Hearts.

Deal the cards around, two at a time. The player on the dealer's left leads for the first trick.

There are no trumps. Each player must follow suit if he can. If he cannot follow suit, he may play any card he chooses. The highest card of the suit led wins the trick. (The cards rank in the usual order: A-K-Q-J-10-9 and on down.) The winner of each trick leads for the next one.

When all the cards have been played, everyone counts the number of Hearts among the tricks he has won.

The player with the least number of Hearts wins.

If there is a tie, another round is played and its score is added to this one to determine the winner.

For Two Players

Deal thirteen cards to each, and place the remainder of the pack face-down on the table. The player who has not dealt leads. The winner of each trick, when he has gathered it in and laid it aside, draws the top card from the face-down pack and adds it to his hand. The other player takes the next top card, and the winner then leads for the next trick.

And so on through the pack, each player always drawing a card to replace the one he plays. When the pack is exhausted, the remaining thirteen cards in the hand are played.

The one who has captured the least number of Hearts wins.

13. Frogs in the Pond

Here is a game where you must keep your wits about you, for you simply cannot afford to forget which high cards *have* been played!

Although Frogs may be played by any number, from two to six, it is best as a partnership game for four.

If there are four players, remove two Deuces from the pack, and deal ten cards, two at a time, to each player, and ten in a pile face-down. These are the Frogs in the Pond. (If three play, use the full pack, and deal thirteen cards to each and thirteen to the Frogs pile. If five play, remove the four Deuces, and deal eight cards to each and eight Frogs. Always the cards must be evenly divided among the players and the Frogs pile.) Everyone picks up his cards and holds them fanshape.

The object is to score 100 points by winning cards that count toward game.

Each	Ten	counts	10
"	Five	"	5
"	Ace	"	4
"	King	"	3
"	Queen	"	2
"	Jack	"	1

These count for the side (or player if you are not playing partners) that wins them in tricks taken.

There is no trump. The highest card of the suit led wins the trick, and the cards rank in the usual order: A-K-Q-J-10-9 and on down. Everyone *must* follow suit if he can. Anyone who "revokes"—fails to follow suit when he can—loses 10 points from his score. If he cannot follow suit, he may play any card.

The player on the dealer's left leads for the first trick. (If he has an Ace he will lead it, hoping his partner may have a Ten or a Five of that suit to throw on the Ace, to count toward game; or perhaps one of the opponents may have no card in that suit except a Ten or a Five, which he will have to play.)

The winner of each trick, as he takes in the cards won, takes also the *top* card of the Frogs pile. He may look at it, but he must not let anyone else see it, not even his partner. He puts it, not in his hand, but with the cards he has won, which are laid face-down beside him. He then leads for the next trick.

The winner of the next trick takes the next Frog (the top card of the pile), looks at it himself, and places it face-down with the cards won. Then he leads for another trick.

And so on—always one Frog for each trick won. And the Frog is never added to the hand.

When all the cards are played, each side counts the points it has won, and the score is marked down. Then the cards are shuffled, cut, and dealt for the next round, the deal passing to the player on the left of the one who dealt before.

The first side (or player if you are not playing partners) to reach 100 points wins the game.

(Sometimes the game is played with Tadpole. Whoever has the Jack of Spades, when the cards are counted for game, has 10 points deducted from his score.)

14. Twenty-Nine

This is fun as a partnership game for four players. But it can be played by three, four, five, or more, each fighting for himself. (If three play, remove one Ten from the pack, and the last trick will not total 29, but 19. If five play, remove one Ten and one Nine; and the last trick will total 10.)

The object is to win as many cards as possible, by reaching the total 29 in adding the number-values of the cards. For example, one trick might contain only a Ten, a Ten, and a Nine, another trick an Eight-Seven-Ten-Four. Each of the face-cards (King, Queen, Jack) counts 1, as does an Ace.

For four players the full pack is used. Deal the cards around, two at a time. Everyone picks up his hand and holds it fanshape. The play is always in turn to the left. You do not have to follow suit, but may play any card at all.

Suppose Dan (the dealer) and Betty are playing partners against Billy and Nancy.

Billy, on Dan's left, begins by leading any card—a Ten, say. If Betty plays a Nine or Ten (making the total 19 or 20), it will be possible for Nancy, her opponent, to take the trick by completing the total 29. So Betty plays a smaller card, hoping, when Nancy has played, her partner Dan can complete the 29.

The player who reaches exactly 29 takes the trick, no matter how many cards—three, four, five, or more —have been played on it. And *the next one on the left* leads for the next trick. The cards won are laid aside, to count toward game.

Each player, as he plays his card, must announce the total it makes—"Nine," "Thirteen," "Twenty-one," "Twenty-nine."

No one may play a card that takes the total beyond 29. But he must play some card—if the total is 27, and he has no Deuce, but a 1 (an Ace, King, Queen or Jack), he must play it and say, "Twenty-eight," even though he knows the next player, his opponent, probably has a 1 and will take the trick.

When the eight tricks have been played (eight times 29), the side with the greater number of cards wins the game.

(If, as almost never happens, someone cannot play any card because the total would go beyond 29, the game ends, and the side that has then won the greater number of cards is the victor.)

15. Giggle a Bit

Any number may play this "word game"—and keep a straight face if they can!

The object is to capture the greatest number of cards.

If there are three players, deal six cards to each; if four players, deal five cards to each; if five or six are to play, four cards apiece will be enough. Lay the remainder of the pack aside, not to be used.

Everyone, without looking at his cards, stacks them face-down in front of him. The play is always in turn to the left.

Bob, the dealer, begins by saying something like this: "Henry went for a walk along a country road. He saw—" *After* he says "saw" he flips the top card of his pile over on the table, face-up. And this is won by the first player (including Bob) to say *two adjectives and a noun* beginning with the *same letter* as the name of the card.

(For example, for a Ten, a Three, or a Two, "a tiny tiresome tadpole" would do; for an Eight, "an elegant elongated elephant"; for a Queen, "a queer quarrelsome quail." Nearly everyone will be caught when a king turns up, for they will be apt to say "a cute cold crab," which of course will be wrong, as those words do not begin with K; "a kind kissable kangaroo" would be all right. The noun does not have to be an animal, of course; it may be anything.)

The one who wins the card (by being the first to finish three correct words) lays it aside, to count for him toward game. It is not used again in play. If two or more players shout correct words at precisely the same time, no one takes the card. It remains on the table and goes to the one who wins the next card.

Evan, on Bob's left, now continues the story of Henry on the country road by saying: "He went on, and saw—" Evan flips over his top card, so all can see it at the same time, and the first one to shout two adjectives and a noun beginning with that letter gets the card and lays it aside.

Joan, next to Evan, now says: "He went on, and saw—" and flips over her top card.

And so on around and around the table, until all the cards have been turned over and each won by someone. No card must be turned until after the word "saw," and then it must be turned quickly.

The player who has the most cards wins the game.

If two players should have the same number, deal each of them two cards off the unused pack; and they play as before, only this time they must say *four* adjectives and a noun!

When the game has been played often and the words come too easily, vary it by using the *second* letter of the card's name instead of the first letter.

♠　♦　♥　♣

For very young players, only one adjective and a noun may be used ("a sad sailor" would do for a Six or a Seven; "a jolly Junebug" for a Jack; "an eatable eagle" for an Eight.) Or no adjective at all, only a noun, if the players are very, very young.

16. My Ship Sails

This is a very easy game, for three, four, five, or more players. Children who know nothing at all about cards will enjoy it, and it is a good game, also, for very young players.

The object is to be the first to have your cards all of the same suit.

Deal seven cards, one at a time, to each player, and lay aside the remainder of the pack, not to be used. Everyone picks up his cards and holds them fanshape. The play is always in turn to the left.

Glen, the dealer, begins. He holds more Clubs, say, than anything else, so he will try to get seven cards of that suit. He takes any one of his cards, not a Club, and lays it *face-down* in front of Dave, the player to his left.

Dave, who is going to try for seven Hearts, puts a card he does not want, face-down in front of Jean, on his left; and *then* he picks up and adds to his hand the card Glen has given him. If it is a Heart, so much the better; if not, he will get rid of it when his turn comes again.

Jean puts a card face-down in front of Dorothy, and then picks up the card Dave has given her and adds it to her hand. So the play goes round the table, each one always putting one card face-down in front of the next player *before* looking at the card he has received.

The first player to get seven cards of the same suit cries, "My ship sails!" He shows his hand and wins the game.

Sometimes Dave gets seven Hearts and Jean on his left gets seven Spades immediately afterward, before Dave has noticed his all-Hearts. The first one to cry, "My ship sails!" wins.

Of course, nobody must ever tell what suit he is saving. That is part of the fun, when two try to get seven cards of the same suit, not knowing that the other one is collecting them, too.

17. Stop-and-Go

Although "Stop-and-Go" sounds like an up-to-date traffic signal, this is really an old, old French game. It is also called Sequence.

Any number may play. If there are four players, deal twelve cards, one at a time, to each player, and lay the remaining four cards aside, face-down, for Stops. (If three play, deal fifteen cards to each, and seven Stops. If five play, deal nine cards to each, and seven Stops. If six play, deal eight cards to each, and four Stops.)

The object is to be the first to get rid of your cards, by building up in sequence (4, 5, 6, 7) of *the same suit* to a Stop.

Everyone picks up his cards and holds them fan-shape, and the play is always in turn to the left.

Billy, on the dealer's left, begins by playing any card face-up in the center of the table, naming its denomination. If it is the Seven of Spades, he says, "Seven."

Nancy, on his left, plays the Eight of Spades, if she has it, and says, "Eight." If she does not have it, she loses a chance to play a card. She must say, "Pass," and the next one who can, plays the Eight of Spades, saying, "Eight."

(Of course, this card may be face-down among the Stops. In that case, each one in turn will say, "Pass," and Billy again must "Go" by beginning another sequence, playing any card he chooses.)

Whenever a Stop is reached, the player of the last

card is the one to Go—begin the new sequence.

All cards are left face-up on the table when they are played, whether a Stop is reached or whether the entire suit is played out.

If Nancy can play the Eight of Spades on Billy's Seven, the next one who can, plays the Nine; then the Ten, Jack, Queen, King.

The King is always a Stop. The one who plays it begins a new sequence, either with the Ace of the same suit, or with any card of any suit.

It is wise to begin a sequence with an Ace, as that is the only way you can get rid of it, for it cannot be played on the King, because the King is a Stop. (If you hold both the King and the Ace, you can end one sequence with the King and begin another with the Ace; but you cannot play the Ace on someone else's King.)

If Billy plays the Ace and also holds the Deuce, he must play it also, immediately after the Ace. And if Nancy holds the Three, Four, and Five, she must play all of them, one after the other.

The first player to get rid of his cards wins the game.

18. Yukon

Yukon, based on an old German game, was played by miners in the Klondike days. And they gave it this name. It makes an interesting and exciting—and often maddening!—game for young players.

It is best as a game for four, playing partners, but it may easily be adapted to two or three.

The Jack of Spades is the *Grand Yukon*, the highest card in the deck. Next in rank are the other Jacks, called *Yukons*, one being no higher than another.

Use the full pack of fifty-two cards (if there are four

or two players; if three play, remove one Deuce.)

Deal five cards, one at a time, to each player, and place the remainder of the pack face-down where everyone can reach it conveniently.

The object is to win tricks containing counting cards, and so be the first to reach 250 points. The cards that count toward game are:

Grand Yukon counts 15 points
Each Yukon   "   10   "
   "   Ten   "   10   "
   "   Ace   "   5   "
   "   King   "   3   "
   "   Queen   "   2   "

The cards rank in their usual order—A-K-Q, etc.—except the four Jacks, which are the highest of all, their suits being disregarded (unless one of them is led.) When any Yukon is played on any trick, the Yukon wins the trick. (If the ♡A is led, the ♣J will win it—or the ♡J or ◊J or ♠J; but a Yukon is played only when its holder cannot follow suit.)

If some trick should contain both a Yukon and the Grand Yukon, the Grand Yukon wins, of course. If two plain Yukons are played on one trick, the first one played wins. (If the ◊A is led, the ♡J is played, and then the ♠J, the Grand Yukon wins the trick. But if the ◊A is led, the ♡J is played, and then the ◊J, the ♡J, being the first played, wins the trick.)

If one of the Yukons should be *led* (which rarely happens), the other players must "follow suit or play a Jack." (If the ♣J is led, each of the other players must play a Club if he has one; if he has no Club, but has a Jack, he must play it, and if it is the Grand Yukon, this wins the trick.)

It is the one rule, *Follow suit or play a Jack,* that

makes Yukon an exciting game. You *must* follow suit
—not even the Grand Yukon may be played if you can
follow suit; and you *must* play a Jack if you cannot
follow suit. Of course, if you have neither the suit led
nor a Jack, you play any card—a Ten if it will be your
partner's trick, and a worthless card if the opponents
will get it.

When the five cards apiece have been dealt around,
the player on the dealer's left leads for the first trick.
A small card is usually the best first-lead.

There is no trump. Each player must "follow suit
or play a Jack." The highest card of the suit led wins
the trick, unless a Yukon has been played on it.

The winner of each trick takes it in and lays it aside,
and then he draws the top card of the face-down pack
and adds it to his hand. Then each player in turn to
the left draws the next top card. This keeps five cards
always in the hands—one is drawn for every one
played. When the pack is exhausted, the five cards in
the hands are played out.

The winner of each trick, after everyone has drawn
a card, leads for the next trick.

When all the cards have been played, each side
counts its score—the values of the Jacks, Tens, Aces,
Kings, and Queens won—and marks it down.

The cards are then dealt by the next player on the
left for another round.

The first side to reach 250 or more points (when the
card score is counted at the end of any deal, and not
during the play of the hand) wins the game.

If both sides have passed 250, the higher score wins.
If there is a tie, the side holding the "Yukon digger"
(Ace of Spades) wins.

19. Old Maid

Any number of brave people may play this old, old game.

Remove the Queen of Clubs and play with the remainder of the pack. Deal the cards around, one at a time. If some players have one more card than others, it does not matter.

The object is to get rid of your cards as quickly as possible, by getting *pairs* (two Eights, two Aces, two Jacks).

Hold your cards fanshape. If you have any pair, remove the two cards from your hand and lay them face-down on the table. If you have three of a kind, only two may be discarded; if four of a kind, all four are discarded, for they are two pairs.

When all players have discarded all pairs they hold, the play begins. It is always in turn to the left.

The dealer draws any one card (he sees only its back and does not know what he is getting) from the fan-spread hand of Cloyd, the player on his left. If he can use the card to form a pair with one he holds, he lays the pair face-down on the table, thus ridding his hand of two cards; but he does not have another turn. If he does not match any card he holds, he must add the card he draws to those in his hand—hoping for better luck when his turn comes on the next round.

Cloyd now draws a card from Ruth, on his left—and lays down a pair if he can. Ruth then draws from Ann, on her left. And so on around and around the table.

Finally all the cards have been paired and laid down except one Queen. The holder of that, alas, is to be an Old Maid. Or an Old Bachelor!

20. Go Fishing

The old, old game of Authors seems much more fun when you call it Go Fishing.

Any number from three to six or eight may play.

The full pack is dealt out, two cards at a time. If some players have one more card than others, it does not matter.

The object is to get the greatest number of "sets" of four cards—four Jacks, four Eights, four Threes, four Kings.

Everybody picks up his cards and holds them fan-shape. If anyone has a set of four, he lays them, stacked face-down, on the table in front of him. Then the play begins.

Richard, on the dealer's left, asks any player at the table for a card, naming both its *denomination* and its *suit*. But Richard *must* hold at least one card of that denomination himself. For instance, if he asks for the Six of Hearts, he must hold in his hand at least one Six; if he asks for the Ace of Spades, he must hold at least one Ace.

If Richard asks Dorothy, and she has the card, she must give it to him. And then he may ask her, or anyone else, for another card. But if Dorothy does not have the card called for, the turn passes to her, and she "goes fishing" for some card she needs to build up a set of four. She may ask Richard or anyone else at the table.

The player who does not have the card he has been asked to give up always has the next turn to go fishing. And he keeps on asking for cards as long as he gets the one he calls for. But he must never ask for any card unless he holds one or more of that denomination himself.

Whenever a player gets a set of four cards, he lays the set, stacked face-down, in front of him.

The player with the greatest number of sets shows that he is the best fisherman, and wins the game.

If two players should have the same number of sets, another game can be played, and its score added to this game, to decide who is the best fisherman.

♠ ◆ ♥ ♣

Very young players can make the game easier by getting a *pair* instead of a set of four, and laying the pair down. They do not name the suit, but merely, "Mary, give me a Nine," or, "John, give me an Ace."

TWELVE GAMES OF SOLITAIRE

21. Pirate Gold

Pirate Gold is an easy game of Solitaire, for very young players. It will fail only about once in four or five times—which is not often enough to be discouraging.

Shuffle the pack, and, holding it face-down in your hand, deal a row of five cards face-up, no two cards touching. Below them, not overlapping, but quite separate, deal another row of five cards face-up.

These ten cards are the Pirate's gold-pieces, and you are the Pirate who will stack up each pile from the treasure-chest pack in your hand. Some piles will grow very high. Some may have few treasures added.

The object is to cover, by dealing two cards from the pack, every *pair* that appears on the table. If there should be no pair at all in the ten cards you have dealt out, you lose the game at once, and must pick up the cards, shuffle the pack over again, and deal out ten more. (This rarely happens.)

If, in the Pirate's layout, there should be two alike (two doubloons, perhaps, or two pieces-of-eight!) cover each card of the pair with a card dealt face-up from the pack in your hand. If there should be more than one pair, cover all the pairs.

This will create a new pair, or perhaps two or more pairs. Cover by dealing from the pack. And continue until all the cards have been dealt to cover pairs.

If you can do this, you win the game. But if at any time there should be no pair on the table to be covered, you lose.

22. Pyramid

This is a fascinating form of Solitaire. It requires a good deal of planning ahead; yet it is not at all difficult to play. And when you win you have a delightful sense of having been ever so clever to make those cards work out just right!

Deal out twenty-eight cards face-up, in the form of a pyramid, with seven horizontal rows, each overlapping the one above—as shown in the illustration. Hold the remainder of the pack in your hand, face-down.

The object is to remove all the cards in the Pyramid, by making combinations of *two* cards (only two) totaling 13—such as a 6 and 7, a 10 and 3. Jack counts 11, so it is removed with a 2. Queen counts 12, so it is combined with an Ace. The King, equaling 13, is removed alone.

The two cards that make 13 need not be in the same suit.

Only a card that is fully uncovered, with no card overlapping it, or partly overlapping it, may be used.

When the Pyramid is laid out, begin by removing any of the bottom-row cards that total 13, including any King. If two cards removed in this way uncover *completely* a card in the row above, it may then be used. (If a Nine partly covers a Four, and the Four will be free by removing the Nine, that combination may not be used, for both cards must be free to begin with.)

When no further cards can be removed, turn to the pack in your hand. Look at the top card. If you can use it to make 13 with any uncovered card in the Pyramid, do so, and remove them both to your discard pile of 13's.

If you cannot combine this top card of the pack with one in the Pyramid, lay it face-up on the table to begin a Boneyard pile. The top card of the Boneyard may be used at any time.

Look at the next top card in your hand, and use it to combine with and remove another card from the Pyramid, or if that cannot be done, place it face-up on top of the Boneyard.

And so on through the pack in your hand. If by that time you have not removed all cards in the Pyramid, you may turn the Boneyard over, and go through it, one card at a time, as you did with the original pack. The Boneyard may be turned over in this way three times, but it must not be shuffled.

If by that time you have not removed all cards in the Pyramid, the game is lost. But you *may* be able to win without turning the Boneyard over even once.

23. Montana

Some children who play Montana consider it an absorbing game, and others do not like it at all! It requires a long time, so do not begin it unless you have an hour or more to while away.

Deal out the entire pack, all the cards face-up, in four horizontal rows of thirteen cards each, no two cards touching.

The object is to rearrange the cards so that each row will have all cards of one suit, and in order, reading from left to right: 2-3-4-5-6-7-8-9-10-J-Q-K. It does not matter which suit occupies which rows.

When the cards are laid out, remove the four Aces and lay them aside. That will leave four vacant spaces in the field.

Now begin the rearranging. Place in each vacant space the card of the *same suit* as the card on the *left* of the space, and *one number higher* than that card.

Suppose a left-hand corner of your field were like this:

The Ace is to be removed, leaving a blank space. Place the ♠5 there, beside the ♠4 (it is the *same suit* and *one number higher*). Move the ◇2 to the left-end space where the ♠5 was. That will begin your Diamond row, with the 2 in its correct position.

Put the ◇3 in the space created by moving the ◇2, and the ◇3 will be in its correct position.

In the space left by moving the ◇3, place the ♣7. And so continue to fill spaces as they occur, always with the card that is one number higher than the card on the left, and of the same suit as that card.

When a space occurs to the right of a King, it cannot be filled, for there is no higher card. This space must remain blank.

As soon as a space occurs at the left end of any row, a 2 should be placed in it. And once a 2 is in position as the first card of a row, it may not be shifted again. If it is a Heart, that must become the Heart row; if it is a Spade, that must be the Spade row.

If a 2 should be *dealt* as the first card of any row, it may be moved to the left-end position of another row, but a 2 that is *placed* may not be shifted.

When no further move can be made, because all the vacant spaces are on the right of Kings, leave on the table all cards that are in their correct positions, gather up all the other cards, including the four Aces, shuffle them thoroughly, and deal them out in order, first filling the top row until it has thirteen cards, then filling the second row, then the third and fourth rows.

Now remove the four Aces once more, and begin again to shift the cards, getting as many more as possible into their correct places.

Once again, when you are blocked by having all

four spaces on the right of Kings, you may gather up the cards that are not correctly placed, shuffle them with the four Aces and deal them out as before. Remove the Aces, and if this time you cannot shift all cards into place, you lose.

But if you succeed in getting all twelve cards of one suit in each row, and in regular order from 2 to King, you win Montana.

24. Lazy Boy

This is an easy form of Solitaire for those who like to win almost every time.

The object is to build *up* on the Aces to the Sevens (A-2-3-4-5-6-7) and *down* on the Kings to the Eights (K-Q-J-10-9-8), always in the same suit.

When the pack has been shuffled, deal off three cards and place them in a stack face-up, with only the top card showing. If it is an Ace or a King, remove it and place it on the table for one of the foundations to build on. If you do remove it and can use, for a foundation or in building, the card it uncovers, do so.

Deal off three more cards and place them face-up on top of the others. Use the top card if you can, and any it uncovers. Then deal off three more and place them face-up on the stack.

Continue through the pack in this way, three cards at a time, laying aside all Aces and Kings when they appear, and building up on the Aces and down on the Kings.

When you have been through the pack in your hand, turn over the face-up stack and, without shuffling, run through it, three at a time, forming a new face-up stack and using every top face-up card you can.

Continue turning over the stack and going through it three cards at a time. If when you do this you are unable to use a single card, you lose. But nearly always you will win.

25. Round the Clock

No skill is required to play this simple form of Solitaire. Whether you win or lose depends solely upon the way the cards fall; yet at times the game becomes quite exciting.

Deal in a circle twelve stacks of four cards each, all face-down, and another stack of four cards face-down in the center of the circle.

The twelve stacks represent the figures on a clock-face (I, II, III, and on around) and they also represent the numbers on the cards (Ace, 2, 3), Jack XI, and Queen XII. The four cards in the center are the King pile.

The object is to have all the cards of the clock in their correct places, face-up, before the King pile is completed—the four Aces face-up in the I pile, the four Deuces in the II pile, the Threes in the III pile, and so on.

Begin with the Ace pile (the I on the clock-face). Turn over the top card and put it, *face-up*, at the *bottom* of its correct pile. If it is a 9, put it face-up under the IX pile. Then take the top card of the IX pile and put it where it belongs; if it should be a Queen, put it face-up beneath the XII pile, and take the top card of the XII (Queen) pile and put it in its right place. Any King goes face-up beneath the center pile.

If the game works out, you will have, at the end, all the cards in their correct positions, from the four Aces on the one o'clock pile to the four Queens at high noon.

If four Kings should be turned up before the other piles are completed, the game ends and you lose.

26. Spread Eagle

Spread Eagle is one of the old, old games of Solitaire that now is almost forgotten.

Remove the four Aces from the pack and place them in the center of the table, in a vertical row, for the Eagle's body.

After removing the Aces, shuffle the remainder of the pack and deal all the cards face-up. First a *vertical* row of six cards to the right of the Aces, to begin the

Eagle's right wing. Then a similar row to the left of the Aces, for his left wing.

Deal another vertical row of six cards on the right, the *side* edges *overlapping* the six cards in the first row. Deal a similar row on the left wing, the side edges overlapping the six already dealt there. Then deal on the right wing a row of five, overlapping the preceding row; then a similar row of five on the left wing. Then deal a row of three on the right, three on the left; two on the right, two on the left; two on the right, two on the left—all with side edges overlapping the preceding row.

```
OOOOOO  A  OOOOOO
OOOOOO  A  OOOOOO
  OOOO  A  OOOO
   OOO  A  OOO
   OOO     OOO
    OO     OO
```

(*Side* edges of cards overlap)

The object is to build up on each Ace, with cards in sequence (Ace, 2, 3, 4, up to King) of the same suit.

Only the outside (fully uncovered) cards in the Eagle's wings may be used—six outside cards in the right wing and six in the left wing. If any of these should be a 2, place it at once on the Ace of the same suit. Then a 3, and so on up.

To uncover a card in either wing that has another card overlapping it, you may "build down" on the wings—"down" in sequence, but "outward" in direction. The outside card (the card that is fully uncovered) of any horizontal column may be moved to the

outside position of another column in the same wing.
But it must be placed on a card of a *different color* and
one number higher (a black 6 and a red 7, a red Jack
on a black Queen). And only one card, the uncovered
one, may be moved at a time. As that uncovers another
card, this card may then be moved in the same way.

When a horizontal column-space is left vacant (all
the cards in it having been used on the Aces in building up, or shifted to other columns in building down),
the vacant column-space may be filled with any outside, uncovered card in the same wing. It is usually
wisest to place a high card, a King if possible, in a
vacant space.

Should you succeed in building the Ace of each suit
up to its King, feather by feather, you have made the
Eagle fold his wings, and you win the game.

27. Four-Leaf Clover

To the eager mind there is more interest in combining cards to total a number than in the mere placing
of one card after another upon an Ace.

Four-leaf Clover is a stimulating "number game,"
not difficult to win for one who is on the alert to combine the greatest number of cards.

First *remove the four Tens* from the pack. They are
not to be used. Then shuffle the remaining forty-eight
cards, and deal, face-up, four rows of four cards each,
no two cards touching. This is the clover-field. Hold
the remainder of the pack in your hand, face-down.

The object is to use up all the forty-eight cards and
remove them from the field by making combinations
in the same suit that total 15 (such as 9-4-2 of Clubs;

7-8 of Spades). Jack, Queen, and King have no num-ber-value, but are removed as a set-of-three when all three, in the same suit, appear in the clover-field at one time (such as Jack-Queen-King of Hearts).

The more cards that can be used to make one 15, the better, as that will leave more spaces in the field for you to fill from the pack in your hand. If part of the field should be:

do not pick up the 6-9 of Hearts, but the 6-A-8, thus removing three cards instead of two.

When the field of sixteen cards is laid out, begin by removing all cards that combined (in the same suit) total 15; or any set of Jack-Queen-King in one suit.

Then from the pack in your hand, fill the spaces in the field. Again remove all the cards you can, in mak-ing 15. Then fill the spaces once more. Continue this —first combining and removing cards, then filling the spaces.

If you find a solid sixteen-card field at any time, and are unable to remove even two cards, the game ends and you lose. But if you succeed in using all the forty-eight cards, in making 15's and sets of Jack-Queen-King, you win the Four-Leaf Clover.

28. Honey-Bee

Bees are far more industrious than you will be when you play this lazy form of Solitaire. For the game depends almost entirely upon the way the cards fall. When they come off the deck just right, it seems much too easy. But when they fall wrong—!

Shuffle the full pack. Then, holding the cards face-down, count off ten cards and place them in a stack face-up on the table, with only the top card showing. This is the beehive.

Deal off the next six cards, placing them in a row face-up, no two cards touching—or in two rows of three cards each if you prefer. This is the flower-garden where the bees will come to get honey—and swarm together in sets of four. Hold the remainder of the pack in your hand, face-down.

The object is to combine all the fifty-two cards in sets of four of a kind—as four Aces, four Sevens—by building them in sets in the flower-garden, and removing each set as it is completed.

With the layout ready, begin to send the bees to the garden. If the top card of the beehive is like any card in the garden, place it on that card. Then the next card in the hive, being uncovered, may be used if it is like any card in the garden.

No card is ever placed on the beehive, as the object is to use up all its cards as quickly as possible. Cards are placed only on the six garden cards.

If two cards in the garden are alike, place one on top of the other, and fill the vacant space with the top card of the beehive. Suppose your layout should be:

Place the ♠5 (the top beehive-card) on the ◇5; if the next beehive-card should be another 5, place it also on the 5-pile. (Or if it is a K, 2, 3, or 10, place it on that pile.) Place the ◇3 on the ♣3, and fill the space (where the ◇3 was) with the top beehive-card.

When all the like-cards have been combined, turn to the pack in your hand and deal off three cards, placing them in a pile face-up, with only the top card showing. This will begin a working-stack. If the top card is like any in the garden, place it on the garden-card, and use the card it uncovers if it is like any in the garden.

Then deal three more off the pack and place them face-up on your working-stack, using the top card if it matches one of those in the garden.

When you get a set of four cards of one kind in the garden, remove it, casting it aside, and fill the vacant space with the top card of the beehive. When there are no more cards in the beehive, fill a vacant-space with the top card of the working-stack.

Go through the pack three cards at a time, placing them face-up on the working-stack and using as many as you can on like-cards in the garden, in building sets of four. Then turn over this stack, and go through it three cards at a time. It may be turned over as many times as you choose, but it must not be shuffled.

Should you go through it without being able to use a single card that is turned up, your bees refuse to go seek honey and you lose the game. But if you make them all gather in the garden in sets of four, you win.

29. Klondike

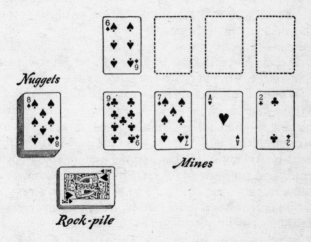

Nuggets

Mines

Rock-pile

Many years ago the name of this game was Canfield, and a quite different game of Solitaire was called Klondike. But somehow the names of the two games became confused; so this one now is Klondike and the other one Canfield.

When the pack is shuffled, count off thirteen cards

and place them in a pile face-up, with only the top card showing. These are the Gold Nuggets.

Next deal off the top card of the pack in your hand and lay it face-up far in front of you (as the ♠6 in the illustration). This is one of your foundation-cards. Instead of building up on Aces you will build on it. (If it is a 6, you will build up, in the same suit, to King, then A-2-3-4-5.)

This foundation-card is one of the four Money-stacks, to be piled up as rapidly as possible. Whatever this card may be, as soon as the other like-cards appear (if it is a 6, the other 6's; if a Queen, the other Queens) lay them beside it—to be built up on in the same suit.

Having laid out the pile of Nuggets and the foundation-card for the first Money-stack, next deal off four cards, face-up in a row. These are the four Gold Mines, and you *descend* in them, building steps down regardless of color (any 8 may be placed on any 9; any King on any Ace).

Then from the pack in your hand deal off three cards and place them in a pile face-up, with only the top card showing. This is the Rock-pile, where you may find gold to put on the Money-stacks, or rocks to build descending steps in the four Mines.

With the layout completed, make all the plays you can, building up in the same suit on the Money-stacks, or down (in any suit) on the Mines. In the illustration, the ♡A can be placed on the ♣2, overlapping but not covering it, and the ♡K can then overlap the ♡A. The ♠7 can be put on the ♠6, covering it, and the ♠8 on the ♠7. (But not the ♣9 on the ♠8, for it is a different suit.)

To uncover a card in the Mines for use on a Money-stack, either the bottom (fully uncovered) card in a Mines column, or *the entire column*, may be moved onto another column whose bottom card is next-higher. Suppose the four Mines columns, sometime during the play, were:

♢Q	♡8	♢10	♡2
♠J		♢9	♢A
		♣8	♠K
		♡7	

the Q-J column could be placed on the ♠K, thus freeing a column-space (which is always helpful); the entire 10-9-8-7 column could then be placed on the ♠J, thus freeing another column-space. Then, if you wanted to use the ♣8 on a Money-stack, the ♡7 could be placed on the ♡8.

When a blank column-space occurs in the Mines row, it may be filled with the top card of the Nuggets, or of the Rock-pile, or with the bottom card of another Mines column. It is wisest to use the top Nugget card to fill such a blank space. No card is ever placed on the Nuggets pile.

Having made all the plays possible, on the Money-stacks and Mines, deal off three more cards from the pack in your hand and place them face-up on the Rock-pile, with only the top card showing. Use this top card if you can, and any that it uncovers. Then deal three more upon the Rock-pile, and use the top card if you can.

Continue this until the pack has been gone through. Then turn over the Rock-pile and go through it, three cards at a time, forming a new Rock-pile. It may be turned over and gone through any number of times, but it must not be shuffled.

If at any time you cannot use a single card to build further, you lose the game. But if you do not overlook a play—which it is easy to do—you will not find it difficult to win Klondike.

30. Down the Stairs

Down the stairs is one of the few games of Solitaire that can be won every time. Yet the correct shifting of the cards forms an absorbing pastime.

The object is to build down in four columns, from King to Ace, without regard to suit or color (any Queen may be placed on any King; any Jack on any Queen).

The full pack is used. Deal out a row of seven cards, side by side, no two cards touching. Three of these will create working-spaces when the cards are removed, and the other four will become foundation-Kings.

Any of the seven cards laid out may temporarily be placed overlapping any other card that is *higher* (a 5 may be placed on a 6, on a 7, or on any higher card, even on a King).

You may begin by shifting as many or as few of the seven cards as you choose—always onto a higher card —creating vacant column-spaces; but it is wise to move only one or two. Suppose your seven cards were:

 ♠8 ♡5 ♡2 ♢K ♣4 ♢6 ♠J

The King, fortunately, would be in a position as head of a column, to be built down on. Place the 6 overlapping the 8, and the 5 overlapping the 6. That will create two spaces, so do not shift the 4 onto the 5 just yet.

Once one card is placed on another (as the 6 on the 8) a *column* is begun, and then only the bottom, un-covered card may be shifted—to another column or to a vacant space. An entire column may never be moved.

When you have shifted one or two cards in your layout of seven, fill the spaces you have made, by deal-ing off the top cards from the pack in your hand. *All* spaces must be filled before you begin to shift cards again. A card may not be dealt onto a column, but must be placed in a space. No card may be dealt from the pack until there is at least one vacant space in the seven columns.

After filling the spaces with cards dealt from the pack (or the bottom card of another column may be placed in some space, but this is not advisable), shift one or two cards onto other columns, to create spaces for further dealing from the pack.

When a King appears, place it in a space, making it the foundation-card for that column, and building down on it (in sequence but regardless of suit) as rap-idly as you can. When a King column is completed, from the King down to Ace, turn it over, face-down.

In a temporary column (one that does not have a King for the top card), it is best to keep the cards in as nearly consecutive order as possible. For example, suppose your layout were three King-columns com-pleted from K to A and turned face-down, and the other four columns were:

Q	6	7	10
9		5	
		4	

In order to deal another card off the pack, a space must be created. You could place the 6 on either the 9 or the 10, but it is better to get it between the 5 and 7. To do so, you would:

Place 6 on 9; 4 on 10; 5 in the space where the 6 was; 6 on 7; 5 on 6; 4 on 5. This will give you one space. If you want to create another one, you can place the 9 in space; 10 on Q; 9 on 10.

Then you are ready to deal two cards off the pack, hoping that one of them may be the foundation-King.

No matter how long a column may be, you can always reach any card in it by the proper shifting of one card at a time. If the Queen were at the very top of a column, buried beneath the eleven lower cards, it would not be impossible to reach it, although it would require many moves to do so.

Down the Stairs can *always* be won!

31. Idiot's Delight

When Idiot's Delight is played "according to Hoyle," it is much too discouraging, for you can win only about once in fifty or sixty times. This is a simplified form, where the chances are much better—about once in two or three times.

When the pack has been shuffled, deal a Triangle of twenty-five cards, all face-up, and each row *overlapping* the row above it. The first row has nine cards. The next has seven, overlapping the middle seven cards in the first row. Then five, then three, then one—each card overlapping the card immediately above it.

Next deal the Boneyard—nine cards spaced well apart, no two cards touching, and all face-down; then

nine cards on top of them, face-down; then nine cards
on top of those, face-up. That will be nine stacks of
three cards each, the top card only of each stack face-
up.

```
O O O O O O O O O
 O O O O O O O
  O O O O O
   O O O
    O
O O O O O O O O O
```

(Each row *overlaps* the row above it)

The object is to build up on the Aces—Ace, 2, 3, 4,
up to King—in each suit.

Only the completely uncovered cards in the Triangle (the bottom card of each vertical column) and
the nine face-up cards in the Boneyard may be used.
If there are any Aces among these eighteen cards, lay
them to one side, for the foundations to build upon. If
there are any 2's of the same suit as the Aces, use
them; then 3's; and so on.

To uncover a card in the Triangle, any bottom (completely uncovered) card of one vertical column may
be lifted over to the bottom of another vertical column, provided it is put on a card of a *different color*
(red on black, black on red) and *one number higher* (a
5 on a 6, a Queen on a King). You "build down" (in a
different color) in the Triangle, and "build up" (in the
same suit) on the Aces.

As soon as a bottom card in the Triangle is used, the
card beneath it is uncovered and it may then be used.

Any face-up Boneyard card may be used at any

time in building either in the Triangle or on the Aces.
As soon as a Boneyard card is used, turn over immediately, face-up, the card that was beneath it. Do not
wait until you make some play you see in the Triangle,
but turn this card over at once, as it may make a difference in your Triangle play.

When the three cards in a Boneyard stack have
been used, leaving a vacant space, this space remains
vacant; it may not be filled with the top card from
another Boneyard pile. And no card in the Triangle
may ever be placed in the Boneyard.

When there is a vacant column-space in the Triangle, any uncovered card in the Triangle (the bottom card of any vertical row) or any face-up card in
the Boneyard may be placed in the Triangle column-
space. It is usually best to place a Boneyard card in
this space, unless it is the bottom card of its pile of
three, as that permits you to turn face-up the next
card in that Boneyard pile.

If you watch the Triangle carefully, constantly
shifting cards from one column to another in building
down, fill the vacant column-spaces, and use the
Boneyard to help you, this form of Idiot's Delight will
not be difficult to win. But it does require close attention!

You win if you succeed in building the Ace of each
suit up to its King, thus using all the cards in the Triangle and all those in the Boneyard.

♠ ♦ ♥ ♣

The real game of Idiot's Delight, the ever-so-hard
game to win, is played in the same way, but the layout
is different. The Triangle has forty-five cards, and the
Boneyard has only seven.

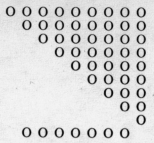

(Each row *overlaps* the row above it)

All the cards are face-up, and in the Triangle each horizontal row overlaps the row immediately above it. Thus when you begin to play there are nine fully uncovered cards in the Triangle (the bottom card of each vertical row) and seven in the Boneyard.

The play is just the same as in the easier form of Idiot's Delight. You build up on the Aces and down (in alternate colors) in the Triangle. The Boneyard cards may be used at any time, on the Aces or in the Triangle. The Triangle cards may never be placed in the Boneyard.

The reason this form of the game is so difficult is because of those long columns of cards on the right. When an Ace or a Deuce is buried there, it is hard to dig it out!

32. Canfield

When this popular game of Solitaire first was played, its name was Klondike, but everyone now calls it Canfield.

At least, they know it by that name, but many of them call it merely "Solitaire"—as if it were the only game of Solitaire ever played!

Deal a row of seven cards, the first card face-up, the others face-down. Then a row of six cards overlapping those above, the first card face-up, the others face-down. Each succeeding row has one card less, and always the first card is face up. The last row, the seventh, will have only one card, face-up.

Hold the remainder of the pack in your hand.

The object is to build up each suit from the Ace to the King.

First look at your layout, the cards you have dealt. If there is an Ace showing, lay it aside for one of your four Ace-foundations. And turn over, face-up, the card that was beneath the Ace.

As soon as a card is face-up it may be used—either

o build *up* on the Aces (in the same suit) or to build *down* on the layout (in sequence and in alternate colors—black on red, red on black). You build down, on he layout, in order to uncover a card so that it may be turned face-up.

All face-up cards in one column may be moved (without disturbing their order) onto another column. But the top card of the ones you are moving must be a different color and the next number lower than the bottom card of the column they are moved onto. (A black 5 heading a column may be placed on a red 6, a red Jack on a black Queen.)

In moving cards from one column to another, *all* face-up cards in that column must be moved together. If one column shows 9-8-7-6, the 6 may not be moved alone onto a 7 in another column, but all four together may be moved onto a 10 of a different color from the 9.)

As soon as a face-down card is uncovered, turn it over, and use it if you can—in building up on the Aces or down in another column.

When any column-space is vacant, only a King may be placed in it. If the King heads a number of face-up cards, all the cards below the King must be moved with it.

When no further moves are possible in the layout, turn to the pack in your hand and deal off three cards, placing them in a pile face-up on the table, only the top card showing. Use the top card of this Boneyard-pile if you can; and if you use it, the next one, being the top card, may be used.

Deal off three more cards from the pack and place them face-up on the Boneyard-pile, using the top one if you can, and any that are uncovered when the top ones are used.

Go through the pack in this way, three cards at a time. Then turn over the Boneyard (but do not shuffle it) and go through it three at a time, forming a new Boneyard as at the beginning. Keep on turning over the Boneyard and going through it, three cards at a time.

If you do this without being able to use a single card, you are blocked, and lose the game. But if you manage to build each Ace up to its King, you win.

Double Canfield

This is a lively game where two players race in playing Canfield.

Ann and Betty sit opposite each other at the table. Each has a full pack of fifty-two cards, and each lays out Canfield as if she were playing alone. But as the Aces appear they are placed on the table between the two players, and both Betty and Ann build up on an Ace. Betty may play the ♡2 on the ♡A Ann has laid out; Ann may then play the ♡3 and ♡4 on it, Betty the ♡5—and so on up.

That is where the excitement comes in, for both may have a ♡5 at the same time, and the one who is the quicker to slap it on the ♡4 is the one who is able to get rid of it.

Except that each player has *eight* Aces to build up on (in the same suit), the game is played like single Canfield. The players may not build *down* on each other's columns, but only on their own columns.

The first one out of cards wins.

China

This is an exciting and fast-moving game of Canfield for two, three, or four players.

It makes a lively party game. But unless your guests are accustomed to playing Canfield they will surely lose the race to China.

Each player has a full pack of fifty-two cards, and deals out the cards as if he were playing Canfield alone. No one begins to play until all the layouts are ready—each one having his twenty-eight cards in place. Then someone says, "China!" and the race begins.

As the Aces appear they are placed in the center of the table where all can reach them. Each player may build on anybody's Aces.

He may build *either up or down* (he may not place an Ace on a Deuce, because Aces must be placed on the table separately, for foundations; nor may he place a King on an Ace, for the Kings must be the final cards; but once the A 2 3 are played, he may put either a 4 or a 2 on the 3).

He may build *regardless of suit* (the ♠4 may be put on the ♡3; the ♣5 on the ♠4; the ♢4 on the ♣5, and so on).

The first one out of cards cries, "China!" and wins the game.

CHINA

TWELVE CARD TRICKS

33. Eagle Bright

While this is one of the simplest of all tricks, anyone who does not know it will be decidedly puzzled.

When you have shuffled the pack, put it face-down on the table. Then have someone draw any card from it, look at the card, and show it to everyone but you; then he must put it *at the bottom of the pack*.

While your back is turned, someone cuts the cards, placing the bottom part on top, so the card selected is somewhere—you do not know where—in the middle of the deck.

Now you take up the cards and, beginning at the top, deal them off, one by one, throwing them face-up on the table. And when you reach the one selected, you astonish your audience by saying, "That is the card!"

How did you know?

You knew the card that was on the bottom of the pack at the beginning, because, having "eagle-bright eyes," you slyly looked at it when you finished shuffling and before you put the pack on the table. When the card you saw on the bottom turned up as you dealt, you knew the very next card would be the one selected, for it was placed immediately below the one you saw.

34. Spelling the Cards

A life-prisoner claims that it took him twenty-seven years to figure out this interesting trick.

Take one complete suit—Spades, say—and discard the remainder of the pack. Arrange your thirteen cards *very* carefully in the following order: 3 8 7 A Q 6 4 2 J K 10 9 5.

Hold the pile of cards thus arranged face-down in your left hand (the 3 will be the top card). Now deal, from off the top onto the bottom, without turning the card over, one card at a time, spelling aloud as you do so, one letter for each card, A C E (A for the first card on the bottom, C for the second, E for the third); then say "Ace," as you turn up the fourth card and lay it on the table face-up, leaving it there. Behold, it *is* the Ace!

Continue spelling, dealing cards from the top of the pile to the bottom, one card for each letter, T W O—laying the next card, as you say "Two," on the table face-up and leaving it there. It will be the 2. Then spell T H R E E, "Three,"—turning up and putting on the table the card that comes after the last E.

And so on through all the numbers. The letters that are *spelled* always represent cards dealt from the top of the pile to the bottom, face-down, and the *words*,

"Four," "Five," etc., always cards that are shown and then left face-up on the table.

When you have passed T E N, "Ten," spell the next card J A C K, "Jack." Then Q U E E N, "Queen." And then you will have only one card left, so it must be K I N G, "King."

35. Needle in the Haystack

For this you must secretly "prepare" the pack, by dividing it into two stacks, one all black cards (Spades and Clubs), the other all red (Hearts and Diamonds).

Laying one stack aside—in your lap or on the table covered carelessly with your left hand, anywhere you can reach it quickly—hold out the other stack, face-down, and have someone draw any card and look at it.

Suppose it is the black half (although of course he does not know that all the cards are black) and he draws the Four of Spades. While he holds the card, you say, "You must write down the name of the card."

This is only to distract his attention, and while he looks about for a pencil, you quickly switch the two stacks, without his seeing you do it, and then say, "Never mind writing it down, if you are sure you can remember it. Put it back in the pack anywhere, while I shut my eyes and turn my head."

You hold out the stack (the red half) face-down, and he slips the card in. You shuffle them thoroughly (being careful to keep their backs toward him, so he cannot see they are all red but his one black card). When they are shuffled, look at the cards yourself, and instantly pick out his card and throw it on the table.

It was easy, of course, because he had drawn a card

from the black stack, and put it back into the red stack—the only black card among them all.

36. Obey the Master

In this trick your friend will think you hypnotize him into drawing precisely the three cards you tell him to draw.

Shuffle the pack, and lift a few cards off the top— the number does not matter, about fifteen or twenty— and lay the remainder of the pack aside, not to be used.

As you lift the cards, distract his attention so you can look quickly at the bottom card of those you lift off. Suppose it is the Five of Hearts.

Spread all your fifteen or twenty cards face-down on the table. Then say, "Give me the Five of Hearts." He picks out any card from those spread on the table and, *without looking at it* (this is important!), hands it to you. You do look at it. (It is the Ace of Spades, but he does not know that.) You lay it face-down in front of you, and say, "Now give me the Ace of Spades."

He chooses another card and hands it over unseen. You look at it and lay it face-down beside the other one. This card is the Jack of Clubs; so you say, "Give me the Jack of Clubs." He draws another card and gives it to you without looking at it. You see it is the Ten of Clubs, so you say, "I will draw one myself now, and that will be enough. I will draw the Ten of Clubs."

After hesitating over the spread cards, you draw the bottom one—the one on the far left—which you know very well is the Five of Hearts (because you saw it when you lifted the cards off the pack). You place it face-down with the three cards he has drawn.

Now turn over the four face-down cards in front of you, and, behold, they are the very cards you named!

If your friend should draw the bottom card—the only one you know—the trick would be spoiled and you would have to shuffle all the cards and try again.

37. Skip About

Deal three files of seven cards each, face-up and overlapping.

Ask someone to note one of the cards—any card— and tell you which of the three files it is in.

Now pick up each file separately, bunching the cards together in a pile without disturbing their order, and put one pile on top of the other in your hand, face-up, being careful to put in the *middle* the file containing the selected card. (If it was in the first file, pick up the second, then the first, then the third.)

Turn over, face-down, the stack of cards in your hand. Once more deal the cards, without shuffling, face-up in three files, laying out three cards across (one card in the first file, one in the second, one in the third), then three more across overlapping the first three, and so on until the layout looks as it did in the beginning.

Ask your friend to tell you which file his card is in now. Once more gather up the three files, putting his in the middle. Turn the cards over in your hand, face-down, and deal them face-up again in three files, as before.

For the last time he is to tell you which file his card is in. And now you know the card, for it is the *middle* card in that file.

Do not tell him yet, however. It will be more mystifying if you gather up all the twenty-one cards, shuffle them a little, then scrutinize them closely before you pounce upon the right one and display it.

♠ ♦ ♥ ♣

You can vary this trick, and make it even more baffling, by not seeing the faces of the cards yourself at all.

Deal the three files *face-down*. Then, without disturbing their order, hold up each file so your friend can see the cards, but you can see only their backs.

When he has noted one card, and told you which file it is in, gather them all up, face-down, with his file in the middle, and deal them again face-down.

Hold up each file, as before, for him to see which one his card is in. Once more gather them up, with his file carefully in the middle, and deal them again face-down.

Hold the files up for the last time for him to see, and when he has told you the file, gather the cards together, still face-down, his file in the middle.

Then begin to deal the cards off, one at a time, throwing them face-up on the table, but carefully counting them to yourself as you do so. When you reach the *eleventh* card, you can safely say, "That is it!"

38. The Four Thieves

It may require a little practice to hold four Kings fanshape facing the audience and have two cards concealed behind one of the Kings, but a few trials will show you just how to hold them.

Let your audience see you pick out the four Jacks and place them one by one on the bottom of the pack, while you begin your story:

"The pack of cards is a warehouse, and the four Jacks are four thieves who plan to rob it. They all meet in the basement"—as you place them on the bottom of the pack.

"Someone sees the thieves in the warehouse and calls the police. The four Kings are the policemen who hasten to the warehouse." You are now picking out the Kings, letting the audience see that you place each one on top of the pack. But as you place the third King you find, have two extra cards with it, on top of it. They will become the second and third cards from the top of the pack, just below the top King.

(Suppose these two extra cards are the ◊7 and ♣5. When you get all the Kings on top of the pack the cards will actually read, from the top down: K-7-5-K-K-K, but the audience must think they read: K-K-K-K.)

All the time you are going on with your story:

"The police arrive by airplane and land all together on the roof. But in the meantime the four thieves have scattered. This one"—take one Jack off the bottom, show it, and place it anywhere high in the deck, being sure it is not above the sixth card—"goes to the fourth floor. This one"—take another Jack, show it, and put it in the pack a little lower than the other—"goes to the third floor. This one"—the same with another Jack—"to the second floor. And this thief goes from the basement to the first floor"—placing it a little above the bottom of the pack.

Be sure to show each Jack, as this will allay suspicion when you fail to show two supposed Kings.

"The four policemen are on the roof, all together." Pick up the top *six cards* (which are supposed to be only four) and spread them fanshape (so only the four Kings will show when you hold the cards up with their backs to you. The two plain cards must be hidden completely behind the second King.

The audience sees the four Kings spread fanshape and sees you then place them all on top of the pack—the roof; and all the time you are going on with your story, which partly distracts their attention from the cards:

"The policemen know they will never catch the thieves if they stay together. They must scatter through the building. One goes to the basement." Lift the top card, show the audience that it is a King, then place it on the bottom of the pack.

"Another policeman goes to the second floor." Place the next top card (which is not a King, so it must not be shown) low in the pack.

"Another to the third floor." Place this one, too, quickly, as it is not a King.

"The fourth decides to remain on the roof, lest the thieves try to escape that way." Lift up the next top card, show the audience it is a King, then replace it on top of the pack.

"Now the four policemen are all scattered, searching for the four thieves."

Put the pack on the table and ask someone to cut it (just one cut), being sure the bottom part of the cut is placed on the top part in the proper way.

"The policeman on the third floor" (or on the second floor if the cut was high in the deck) "saw one of the thieves running up the stairs. He blew his whistle, and all the other policemen rushed to his floor.

"So now they are all together again!"

Turn the pack over, face-up, and lightly spread it on the table—and there are the four Kings, huddled together about midway!

39. One by One

One by One is a "mind-reading" trick.

A new pack of cards is best, where all the cards are straight; in an old pack they are often bent from much handling.

Begin by telling your audience you will name each card by reading the mind of someone who sees it. But you can only do that by first working magic on the card.

Have someone shuffle the pack thoroughly, so you cannot be suspected of having "arranged" the cards.

You are going to hold them behind your back. As they are handed to you, or as you swing them behind you, note the card that is on the bottom—without letting anyone see you do it, of course. Suppose it is the ♣4.

With both hands behind you, take off the top third of the pack (the exact number does not matter), and turn it in reverse, so the bottom two-thirds will be facing the audience, and the top third will face you when you hold the cards in front of you. While you are doing this you can be mumbling some "Hokus-pokus-dommus-nickus" magic formula.

Now with the pack deep in the right hand, the fingers curled well over the cards (to conceal that all of them are not facing the same way), hold the pack out in front of you, the bottom card facing the audience, and say, "Mary is thinking of the Four of Clubs. So that is the card she sees!" (At the same time you note the ♢6 facing you.)

Swing the pack behind you quickly, and while you chant your magic, slip the ♢6 from the top of the pack to the bottom, turning the card as you do so, so it will face in the direction of the other bottom cards.

Hold the pack in front of you, deep in your right hand, and say, "John, your mind is hard to read, but I believe—yes, it *is* the Six of Diamonds!"

(You note the card now facing you is the ♡K.) Behind you again, you switch that card to the bottom, and when you hold the pack out you can say, "This one is easy, because *everybody* is thinking of the King of Hearts!"

And so on, for eight or ten cards, being careful to name the card you put on the bottom, and *not* the card that is facing you at the time!

And be very, very careful that no one peeks behind you while you are working your magic!

40. Turn Around

This trick is easy to learn and easy to remember. It will be great fun to watch your friends struggle with it. Then, when they have tried this way and that, becoming more and more entangled, show them how simple it is by doing it in no time at all!

Even after they see you work it, they probably will fail unless you tell them just where the catch comes in.

Pick out one complete suit except the King and Queen, and arrange the eleven cards in order in three rows, with a space at the end—as in the illustration.

The trick is to move *one card at a time,* into the space that is next to it, and end with the cards completely reversed in order:

```
J   10   9   8
7    6   5   —
4    3   2   A
```

with the space at the end of the middle row this time.

There will always be one space, and only a card that adjoins this space may be moved into it. (The first move must be either the J or the 8, as no other card adjoins the space. If the Jack is moved, the next move must be the 7 or the 10. If the 8 is moved, the next move must be the 7 or the 4.)

The cards may be moved either up or down or across, but not diagonally.

Try this yourself before you read the solution. You will find it a fascinating game. But, like other tricks, it loses much of its interest once you know how it is done!

The solution is quite simple. These are the moves in their correct order:

```
J   10   9   5   6       7   8
J   10   9   5   6       1   2   3   4
J   10   9   5   6       1   2   3   4
J   10   9   5   6       1   2   3   4
J   10   9   5   6       1   2   3   4
J   10   9   8   6       1   2   3   4
J   10   9   8   5       1   2   3   4
                 7   6   5
```

The catch comes toward the end, so be on the alert after you get the 9 in the top row, for the next move will be the 8 (not the 5), and then the 6 (not the 7).

When you have learned to shift the cards quickly, watch someone else try it!

41. The Magic Change

The Magic Change is an excellent trick, easy to perform, yet wholly puzzling.

Hand the pack of cards to someone—Dorothy, perhaps—and say to her, "I shall leave the room. While I am gone, shuffle the pack and cut it. Then think of some *number* from 1 to 14. Count down to that number in the pack; note what card it is—if you think of 9, count down to the 9th card and look at it; if you think of 13, count down to the 13th card. Then replace the cards as they were, so your card is still the 9th or the 13th—or whatever number you thought of."

You leave the room. Dorothy thinks of 6, say, and when she counts down she sees that the 6th card is the Jack of Spades. She leaves it in its position as the 6th card.

You return, take the pack and say to someone else, "While I am out of the room again, Richard, you write down some number from 15 to 20. When I return, I will make Dorothy's card magically change its place, from her number to yours."

Leave the room, taking the pack with you. Now rapidly but very carefully deal off, one by one, and *face-down*, the top *sixteen* cards, placing one on top of the other as you count them off. Then replace the pile of sixteen, in their new order, on top of the face-down pack. These sixteen cards will be exactly reversed. The card that was on top will now be the sixteenth, the former second card is now the fifteenth, and so on.

You return to the room and ask Richard what number he wrote down.

If he says 17, all right. If he says 16, you must slip one card from the top of the pack to the bottom; if 15, two cards from the top to the bottom. If he says 18, slip one card from the bottom of the pack to the top; if 19, two cards from the bottom to the top; if 20, three cards from the bottom to the top.

As your audience will see you do this, you can say, "For luck!" or, "To make it more confusing," or anything of the sort.

Now ask Dorothy what number she thought of.

If she says 6 (and Richard has said 19 and you have put two cards from the bottom on top), give a few taps on top of the pack and say, "Card, I command you to skip from Dorothy's number to Richard's!"

Then to Dorothy: "Now I will count from 6 to 19, and there it will be!"

Count aloud, "Six"; then throw the first card face-up on the table as you say "Seven"; then the next card for "Eight"; then "Nine," and so on. (Be sure to *say* the number thought of, but begin your count with the next number *after* that; if Dorothy's number was 10, say "Ten," and count the first card "Eleven.")

Count all the numbers aloud as you deal off the cards, and when you reach "Eighteen"—the one before Richard's number—you can pause dramatically and say, "The next one, if it skipped down when I told it to, will be Dorothy's card." Turn it over as you say, "Nineteen"—and lo, it is the Jack of Spades!

Dorothy and everyone else saw it as the 6th card.

How could it become the 19th? You could not have "placed" it when you had the pack out of the room, because you could not possibly know what card Dorothy saw, nor what number she thought of, nor what number Richard wrote down.

It is all very baffling!

42. Poke Sank

This is sometimes called the Wandering Pairs, and there are two or three ways of performing it. *Poke Sank Lent Play Toys* seems the easiest to remember, so it will be given first.

Fix those five words firmly in your mind, and picture them printed on the table, one beneath the other:

P O K E
S A N K
L E N T
P L A Y
T O Y S

The trick is to deal out twenty cards in twos (called pairs, although the two cards will not be alike—one may be the ♢5 and the other the ♣9), have someone note *any one pair* (not any two cards) as you lay it face-up on the table, and when you have dealt out all the pairs you will tell him the two cards he has chosen.

Begin by saying, "I will deal off eight or ten pairs," as if the number did not matter at all, but actually it is very important for you to make it precisely ten pairs.

There are ten pairs of letters in *Poke Sank Lent Play Toys,* and each pair will represent two cards you deal out. The first pair you deal must be placed where the two P's are—one card at the upper left corner of your layout, and the other far enough below it to get in a card for S *(Sank)* and L *(Lent)* later on.

After the first pair is dealt, wait a minute before you deal the next pair. This will keep your audience from confusing the first two cards with the second two, and it will give you a chance to picture in your mind just where the next pair will be dealt, for they will be placed where the two O's are—one where the O is in *Poke,* and the other for the O in *Toys.*

Hesitate after this pair, also, and picture the position for the next two cards—to be placed where the two K's are.

Hesitate again, and then deal the two E's. Then the two S's, the two A's, N's, L's, T's, and Y's.

As you lay each two cards face-up on the table, it looks as if you were placing them here, there, anywhere, but of course you are following a very careful system.

The numbers under the letters in this table show the order in which you deal the cards off the pack, 1-2 being the first pair, 3-4 the second, and so on.

P	O	K	E
1	*3*	*5*	*7*
S	A	N	K
9	*11*	*13*	*6*
L	E	N	T
15	*8*	*14*	*17*
P	L	A	Y
2	*16*	*12*	*19*
T	O	Y	S
18	*4*	*20*	*10*

Hesitate briefly between each pair, giving your audience time to note well the pair that is chosen. It is really better for them to write down the two cards they select, for then they will not confuse them with a later pair and believe that you are wrong when you name the two cards they chose.

When you have dealt the final two cards (Y-Y), say, "That is enough. Now tell me *what rows* your pair is in, and I will tell you what cards they are."

If someone says the second and fourth rows, you spell those two rows in your mind (*Sank* and *Play*) and know at once that the only like-letter in the two words is A, so his pair will be the two cards in the position of the two A's—the second card in the *Sank* row and the third card in the *Play* row.

If he says the third and fifth rows, it must be the last card in the *Lent* row and the first in the *Toys* row —because only T-T are alike in those two rows.

One good thing about this trick is that any number of people (up to ten) may choose pairs as you deal them out; and you can name them all, one after the other, when each has told you the rows his pair is in.

♠　♦　♥　♣

Another way to perform the trick is to have four rows with five-letter words. You may take your choice between four English words and four Latin words, the trick otherwise being the same as *Poke Sank Lent Play Toys*.

In the five-letter words, however, you must say, "Tell me what *row* or *rows* your pair is in," and it is not quite so mystifying when the two cards are in the same row. The Latin words are better than the English, as they have no two cards of a pair side-by-side. But the English words are much easier to remember, and that is an important part of the trick.

The two sets of five-letter words, and the order in which the cards are dealt, are:

U	S	U	A	L		M	U	T	U	S
1	3	2	5	7		1	3	5	4	7

S	H	E	E	R		D	E	D	I	T
4	9	11	12	13		9	11	10	13	6

C	H	A	F	F		N	O	M	E	N
15	10	6	17	18		15	17	2	12	16

C	O	L	O	R		C	O	C	I	S
16	19	8	20	14		19	18	20	14	8

43. Turnstile

Not everyone knows that in every pack there are many cards whose small numbers in the corners (4, 5, 6) are printed unevenly as to margins—at one end of the card the number is closer to the side edge than at the other end.

Pick out four or five cards whose margins are noticeably different, and lay them face-up side by side on the table—being careful to make all narrow margins on the left-side of the cards.

Say now to someone, "While my back is turned and my eyes are closed, turn one of these cards around, so the top of it will be where the bottom is now. I will tell you which card you moved."

When you turn back and open your eyes, you can tell instantly, for you will see one of the cards with its narrow margin on the right.

To mystify him further, you can take four more cards and tell by the way the pips are pointed. In most of the Hearts, Clubs and Spades, it is very easy to tell one end of a card from another by the way the pips are printed, some pointing up and some down.

Then take four more cards whose pips are exactly alike top and bottom (any Diamond except the 7; or the 2, 4, 10, and face-cards in the other suits) and tell again by the margins. But be sure there is enough difference in the side margin for you to detect the change!

44. Fortune Telling

Of course, nobody really *believes* in fortune-telling. But is fun to make believe.

Hundreds of years ago someone pretended he could "read" the cards. He made up everything as he went along, but he soon ran out of ideas and found himself saying the same things over and over. So he gave each card a certain meaning, and in that way, as he saw the cards, he could think of different things to say.

The cards have no meaning at all, of course. You can no more really tell fortunes with them than you could with so many pieces of blank paper. No one must truly believe anything you say. But it *is* fun as a "Let's pretend" game, and the more mysterious you make it, the jollier it will be.

This is the way you "tell fortunes":

Only twenty-eight cards are used, the seven highest of each suit: A-K-Q-J-10-9-8. Shuffle them, and have the one whose fortune you are telling cut them with the left hand. (It *must* be the left hand!)

Holding the pack face-down, count off six cards and place them, still face-down, on the bottom of the pack. Then turn up the *seventh* (seven is a magic number!) and place it face-up on the table, for the first fortune-card. Deal six more to the bottom of the pack, and turn up the seventh, placing it face-up on the table beside the first card.

Continue this until you have seven cards spread out in front of you. Lay the remainder of the pack aside, and you are ready to begin your "reading."

HEARTS:

Ace: The home. (Whatever the card on either side of it says, will happen at home.)

King: A man with red hair will help you in some way.

Queen: A very pretty girl, with blond hair, will prove to be a loyal friend.

Jack: A blue-eyed boy will do something for you when you least expect it.

Ten: A pleasant surprise is coming your way.

Nine: You will quarrel with someone, but you will soon "make up" and be better friends than ever.

Eight: You are soon going some place where there will be many, many children.

CLUBS:

Ace: You will soon receive some money, but it will not be a gift—you will earn it.

King: A dark-haired older boy—a very nice boy—has taken a great fancy to you.

Queen: This is the girl you like best. You and she will spend happy hours together.

Jack: You and a boy with dark hair and brown eyes are going on a short journey.

Ten: This is the "good luck" card. Everything you do in the next few days will be highly successful.

Nine: The friend you like best will prefer you above everyone else.

Eight: An exciting adventure awaits you.

SPADES:

Ace: Among the many young people you know, there are two who will be your lifelong friends.

King: A policeman will be looking for you!

Queen: You know a dark-haired girl who is very jolly and who likes to flatter. You must not believe everything she tells you!

Jack: Beware of a disagreeable boy with black eyes, for he is planning to do you an injury.

Ten: Mild punishment is in store for you, alas.

Nine: A disappointment will make you unhappy, but only for a short time.

Eight: You will hear something that you will not like.

DIAMONDS:

Ace: You will soon receive an important letter.

King: Beware of a certain older boy with blue eyes and fair hair, for he is not your friend.

Queen: A blond girl that you know simply cannot keep a secret, so do not tell her everything.

Jack: A fair-haired boy will tell you some bad news.

Ten: You are going on an unexpected journey, and it will turn out to be a very happy one.

Nine: You expect some money, but you will not receive it—at least, not when you expect it.

Eight: A boy you know will tell you something that will surprise you very much.

When you have laid out the seven cards and are ready to begin your reading, do as all fortune-tellers do—think of something you *know* about the one whose fortune you are telling and bring that into the story.

Suppose you are reading Carol's fortune and know that she is soon going for a visit to her grandmother or her aunt. You can say solemnly, pointing to one of the cards as if you were reading it there: "You are going for a visit to someone who is much older than you."

Or if you know she is going to the seashore, which is some distance away: "You are going on a long journey. There will be trees and water—much water."

Or if her birthday is approaching: "You will soon receive a present that will please you very much."

When you cannot think of *anything* to say, refer to the cards for ideas. But the fortunes that are most fun are those that you make up as you go along, based on things that you really know will happen!

SOME GAMES THAT GROWN-UPS PLAY

45. Rummy

This is one of the most popular games for two, but it may be played, also, by three, four, or five.

The full pack is used. If two are playing, ten cards are dealt to each, one card at a time, and the next card is turned face-up on the table to begin the Discards pile. The remainder of the pack is placed face-down beside it.

The object is to get rid of your cards, by laying face-up on the table in front of you *three of a kind* (such as three Fives, three Kings) or *three of the same suit in sequence,* as:

The Ace may be used at the top of a sequence (Q-K-A), or at the bottom of a sequence (A-2-3), but never in the middle (K-A-2).

Only *three* cards may be laid down at one time—either three of a kind (triplets) or a sequence of three. But when your turn comes again you may play *one* card at either end of a sequence that is on the table—whether it is your own or your opponent's—or you may place the fourth card beside any triplet.

For example, if you have already laid on the table:

then either you or your opponent may lay down either the ♠A or the ♠5 beside this sequence; and when the ♠5 has been played, the ♠6 may then be played (in turn), and on up in sequence.

Or if there should be on the table:

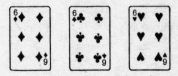

either you or your opponent, when your turn comes, may lay the ♠6 beside the Six-triplet.

Suppose Denis and Janet are playing Rummy, and Denis has dealt.

Janet has the first play. She adds to her hand the face-up card on the table (the one that begins the Discards pile) *if* she can use it to form a combination of three (a triplet or a sequence).

If she cannot use it, she leaves it on the table and draws the top card from the pack and adds it to her hand.

Whichever card she adds to her hand (the Discard or the one she draws), she may now lay down, face-up in front of her, any *one* combination of three cards. She then discards one card, placing it face-up on the Discards pile.

If she has no combination to lay down, she merely discards, after she has drawn a card.

She does not have to lay down a combination she holds, if she prefers not to show it yet, but if she does lay it down, it must be done before she discards. And no matter how many combinations she holds, she may lay down only one each time she draws a card (from either the stack or the Discards pile). If she holds a long sequence, such as:

she may lay down only three of those cards—2-3-4, or 3-4-5, or 4-5-6—playing the others later, one at a time, if she wants to.

After Janet, beginning the game, has drawn a card, laid down a combination, and discarded, Denis draws a card and adds it to his hand. He may draw either the face-up top card of the Discards, or the face-down top card of the stack, whichever he prefers. He will take the one from the Discards pile, of course, if he can use it to form a combination of three.

After he adds the card to his hand, he may lay down one combination he holds (whether it is one just formed with the card he drew, or one which he had in the ten cards that were dealt to him) or he may play a card at either end of Janet's sequence or triplet, if she has one in front of her, and then he must discard one card face-up on the Discards pile. And it is Janet's turn again.

So the game goes on, each player in turn—draws, lays down, discards.

Only one play may be made after each draw—one combination may be laid down, or one card added to a sequence or triplet.

When one player has laid down all his cards—except the one he must discard—he cries, "Rummy!" and wins the game.

If neither one is out of cards when the face-down stack has been gone through, the Discards pile is turned over, face-down, and the game continues, the next one drawing from this stack and beginning a new Discards pile.

♠ ♦ ♥ ♣

If there are three, four, or five players, Rummy is played the same way, the player on the dealer's left having the first play, and then each playing in turn to the left.

If three play, seven cards (instead of ten) are dealt to each. If four or five play, six cards are dealt to each.

46. Casino

Casino has been popular for many, many years. It is very easy to play. Perhaps that is the reason that some grown-ups prefer it to any other game!

Casino is a game for two, three, or four. If there are four players, it is more fun to play partners than for each one to fight for himself.

The full pack is used, and the cards rank in the usual order: A-K-Q-J-10-9 and on down. The Ten of Diamonds is called *Big Casino,* and the Deuce of Spades is *Little Casino*. The object of the game is to win the highest number of points. The player winning:

Cards (the greatest number) .... scores 3
Spades (the greatest number) .... " 1
Big Casino (Ten of Diamonds) .... " 2
Little Casino (Deuce of Spades) .... " 1
Ace (of any suit) .... " 1
Sweep (all cards on the table) .... " 1

Suppose Richard and Ann are partners, playing against Evan and Joan.

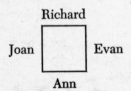

Richard

Joan   Evan

Ann

Richard deals two cards to Evan, two to Ann, two to Joan, two *face-up* in the center of the table, two to himself; then another round of two in the same way; so each player has four cards, and there are four face-up on the table. He places the remainder of the pack face-down.

When this first round of four cards apiece has been played, Richard deals four more to each player, two at a time, but gives none to the table. When they have been played, he deals four more apiece, and so on until the pack is exhausted. None are dealt to the table except the four at the beginning.

Evan, being on the dealer's left, has the first play.

He wants to win all the *cards* he can, all the *Spades* he can, the *Big Casino,* the *Little Casino,* and all the *Aces* he can. He now must play one card (only one) from his hand, and with it he may do one of five things:

(1) *Match* one or more of the face-up cards on the table.

If he holds a 6 and there is a 6 on the table, he may play his 6 on it, and then gather up both of them and place them face-down beside him—not to be used further, but to count toward *Cards* at the end. If there are two 6's he may match them both with his 6, and thus take in the three cards.

The face-cards, King, Queen, Jack, having no number-value, cannot be used in any way except to match.

(2) *Combine* two or more cards on the table to equal one he holds.

If he holds a 9, and there are on the table a 6 and 3 —or a 5-2-2, or any combination that adds to 9—he may play his 9, and gather it in with all the cards totaling 9. Suppose the four cards on the table are:

He lays down his 9, and takes it in, with the 3-A-5, which total 9. Besides now having four cards for his game-pile (the four he has gathered in and laid aside, 9-3-A-5), the Ace itself will score 1 point for him.

(3) *Call* a card or a combination.

If he holds two 10's, and on the table there are:

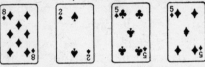

he may stack up the 8-2 and 5-5, play one 10 on them, and call, "Tens," intending to take this pile with his other 10 when his turn comes again. (No player may ever play more than one card at each turn.) Stacked cards are always face-up, and placed near the player.

When cards are stacked no one else may touch any of those cards, to match them or to combine them in some other way. But if another player, before it comes around to Evan's turn again, has a 10, he may play it and take in the entire stack.

If Joan, Evan's partner, has a 10, when it comes her turn she will place it on the stack, and leave it as one more card for Evan to take in. Or if Ann played a 6 on the table, and Joan holds a 4, she will play the 4 and place the 4-6 on Evan's Ten-stack, thus giving her partner two more cards.

When it comes Evan's turn again, he must play his other 10 and gather in his stack, unless he can make some other play that will take in cards. Instead of playing his 10, he may, if he prefers:

Match: Play a Queen from his hand on a Queen someone has played on the table, and take them both in.
Combine: Play a 9 from his hand on a 6-3 and take them in.

Capture: If Ann played a 2, Joan a 4, and Richard stacked the 2-4, played a 6, and called, "Sixes," Evan could capture the stack by playing a 6 on it.

Increase: Play a 3 from his hand on a 7 that has appeared on the table, and increase the size of his Ten-stack by placing the 3-7 on it.

If Evan does any of these four things, he must leave his Ten-stack until his turn comes again, as he may play only one card each turn.

(4) *Build* by stacking one or more table cards *with one played from the hand* to equal a higher card still held in the hand.

If Evan holds a 7 and a 2, and there is a 5 on the table, he may play his 2, stack it on the 5, and say, "Building Seven." No one else may then use the 5 or 2, but if anyone has a 7 he may gather in Evan's stack with it.

Suppose Ann, next to Evan, takes it with a 7. Joan may then play a 4 from her hand on a table 3, and say, "Building Seven," even though she holds no 7, as she is building it for her partner, knowing that he has not played his 7. When Evan's turn comes, he must take it in.

No one may *build* unless he holds the higher card in his hand—a 7 if he is "Building Seven"—except when he builds for his partner, *knowing* his partner holds that higher card.

If no one at all has disturbed Evan's Seven-stack, when it comes his turn again he must do one of these five things:

Take it in by playing his 7.

Increase it, by playing another 7 from his hand (if he holds two), or by playing a 3, say, and combining it with a table 4 and adding them to the stack.

Build it higher if the stack consists of only *one combination* totaling 7. (If he holds a 10, he may play on the Seven-stack a 3 from his hand—or an Ace from his hand and a table 2—and say, "Building Ten." Anyone else with a 10 can then take it before it comes around to Evan's turn again. But no 7 can take it, because it is now a Ten-stack.)

Match a table card with one from his hand, gathering them both in—leaving his Seven-stack until his next turn.

Capture opponent's stack, by playing the card opponent was "building" or "called."

If Evan should fail to do any of these five things, his stack is scattered and the cards are free for any player to use, separately or together.

A stack of *more than one combination* (such as 4-3 and 5-2, "Building Seven") may not be built higher. A *single combination* (such as 3-2-2, "Building Seven") may be built higher by any player who holds the card to raise it and the higher card to take it on the next round.

For example, Evan may play a 3 from his hand on a table 4 and say, "Building Seven." Ann, next, may play on it a 2 from her hand (*not from the table*) and say, "Building Nine," if she holds a 9. Joan, next, may play an Ace on it, and say, "Building Ten," if Joan holds a 10. The first one who plays a 10 may then take the stack.

(5) *Trail.* If the four cards dealt to the table were:

and Evan, who has the first turn to play, finds that he holds these four:

he cannot *match,* nor *combine,* nor *call,* nor *build,* so he must play a card and leave it face-up on the table, for any other player to use. This is called *trailing.* If you must trail, it is wisest to play a small card—but never an Ace nor Little Casino (the Deuce of Spades) if you can avoid it.

When Evan has played, Ann, next on the left, has a turn, then Joan, and on around, each in turn to the left. And each one may do any of the five things—match, combine, call, build, or trail. Or if someone is calling or building, anyone else may capture the stack if he holds the right card.

If anyone plays out of turn, that card is "dead" and must be laid aside until its owner's turn comes. Then he must trail it—play it face-up on the table; he may not use it to take in any cards.

The one who makes the *last play that takes in cards,* after the entire pack has been dealt out, takes any extra cards that are on the table. This is not a Sweep unless all the cards together exactly total the value of the card that is played.

When all the cards have been played, each side counts the number of *cards* it has won. The side with the greater number scores 3 points. If there is a tie, neither side scores. Then each counts its *Spades*, and the greater number scores 1 point.

Then the other scoring is marked:

2 points for the one who has *Big Casino*, 1 for *Little Casino*, 1 for each *Ace*, and 1 for each *Sweep* made during the play. (Sweeps can be remembered by turning one of the cards taken in face-up whenever a sweep is made.)

Sometimes each deal forms a game, and the side with the higher score wins.

Sometimes 21 points are the game. If both sides should have 21 points when the scoring is marked at the end of a deal, the side reaching the total with *Cards* would win over the one reaching 21 with *Spades*, for the points are scored in this order: Cards, Spades, Big Casino, Little Casino, Aces, Sweeps.

Draw Casino

In this form of the game, after the first four cards are dealt to each player, and four face-up on the table, the remainder of the pack is placed face-down where all can reach it; and after each one plays a card, he draws one from the top of the pack, thus always having four cards in his hand.

47. Seven-Up

In the North the game is not always known by this name. There it is usually called High-Low-Jack. But in the South and the West, where it is a favorite, it is called Seven-up.

It is an interesting game for two or three, and an excellent game for four, playing partners.

The object is to win a score of 7 points.

High (the highest trump played) *counts 1.*

Low (the lowest trump played) *counts 1* for the one who plays it.

Jack (of trumps) *counts 1* for the one who wins it in play.

Jack, if turned up for trump in the deal, *counts 1* for the dealer.

Game (the highest total value of cards won in play, counting each Ten as 10; each Ace 4; each King 3; each Queen 2; each Jack 1) *counts 1.*

Gift (when one player "begs" and the dealer gives him 1) *counts 1.*

Suppose Anita and Bob are playing partners against Carol and Dale. Carol, having drawn the highest card, is the first dealer.

She deals six cards, three at a time, to each player, including herself. Then she turns up the next card for trump, and leaves it on top of the deck. (If it is a Jack, it counts 1 point for her.) She places the pack on the table, with the trump card face-up.

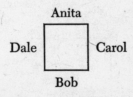

Anita

Dale | | Carol

Bob

Bob, on the dealer's left, is the only one who now looks at his hand. The others leave their cards on the table. If Bob is satisfied to have that suit for trump, the others pick up their hands, and the play begins.

But if Bob (before anyone else has looked at his hand) does not like that suit for trump, he says, "I beg." Carol, the dealer, then looks at her hand, and if *she* wants that suit for trump, she says, "I give you 1." This is called *Gift,* and counts 1 point for Bob's side; the trump and the hands dealt must remain as they are.

But if Carol would rather change the trump than to "give 1" to Bob's side, she places the trump card on the bottom of the pack—Dale and Anita may then look at their hands—and deals out three more cards to each player, including herself; then she turns up the next card for trump. (If it is the Jack of another suit, she scores 1 point for "turning up Jack"—but she does not score if it is the Jack of the suit that has just been refused for trump.)

Suppose the first card turned up for trump were the ♡Q, Bob "begged," and Carol held:

♡A   ♡J   ♡8   ♡2   ♠5   ◇K

she would want Hearts for trump, so she would "give 1" to Bob. But if she held:

she would much prefer to change the trump; so she would put the ♡Q on the bottom of the deck, deal three more cards all around, and turn up the next card for trump.

If the new card turned up is the same suit as the old trump, it is placed on the bottom of the deck, and three more cards are dealt to each player, and the next card turned up for trump. This is continued until a different suit from the first trump is turned up. The hand must be played at this new trump—Bob may not beg again if he does not like the suit.

Each player now weeds out his hand, keeping the six cards he prefers, throwing away the rest. The trump card remains face-up on top of the stack, where everyone may see it during the play.

Bob leads for the first trick. If he holds the Ace of trumps and not the Jack, he will want to lead the Ace, hoping to capture the Jack or the Ten. If his partner Anita holds either of these she will put it on Bob's Ace.

Everyone must either follow suit or trump. He may play a trump if he cannot follow suit. If he has neither trump nor the suit led, he plays any other card. The highest card of the suit led wins the trick, unless it has been trumped. The winner of each trick leads for the next one.

The object in winning tricks is to capture the *Jack of Trumps* (which scores 1) and any cards (Tens, Aces, Kings, Queens, Jacks) that will add up for *Game* (which scores 1).

When all the cards have been played (six by each player), each side counts its Game value. Bob and Anita may have, among all the cards they won:

♣10   ◇10   ◇A   ♠K   ♡K   ♣Q

which would give them a total count of 32. And Dale and Carol may have, among the cards they won:

a total of 30. So Bob and Anita, having the larger number, score 1 for *Game*.

When all the score has been marked down (*High, Low, Jack, Game*), the cards are shuffled and dealt once more—by Bob this time, because he is next on the left of the last dealer; and Dale has the privilege of "begging" or accepting the first trump turned up.

The side that first reaches 7 points wins the game.

If the score should be 5 for each side, at the end of any deal, and if in the next deal Bob and Anita should win *High, Game,* and Dale and Carol *Low, Jack,* Dale and Carol win the game, for the points must be counted in this order: *High, Low, Jack, Game*—and as *Jack* comes before *Game,* Dale and Carol get their two points first.

48. High Five

Many games based on Seven-up are played in different parts of the country. The most popular of all is High Five, which in some sections is called Cinch and in others Double Pedro.

Any number, from two to six, may play, but the

most interesting game is for four, playing partners.

In High Five the Five of the trump suit is called the *Right Pedro*. And the Five of the same color (called the *Left Pedro*) becomes a trump, and ranks between the Five and Four of trumps.

The object is to win 51 points. 14 points can be won on each deal:

High (Ace of trumps) ....counts		1
Low (Deuce of trumps)	"	1
Jack (of trumps)	"	1
Game (the Ten of trumps)	"	1
Right Pedro (Five of trumps)	"	5
Left Pedro (Five of same color)	"	5

These all count for the one who wins them in taking tricks, and not for the one who plays them.

Nine cards are dealt to each player, three at a time. The remainder of the pack is placed on the table, face-down. No trump is turned up, for this is a bidding game. Everyone picks up his cards at once.

Suppose that Ronald and Blanca are playing against Peter and Doris, and Ronald is the dealer.

Peter, on the dealer's left, makes the first bid, knowing that if he gets the bid he may name any suit he chooses for trump. Out of the 14 points that it is possible to make, he bids as many as he feels he can win with his partner's assistance. He will have a chance to bid only once, so he looks his hand over carefully. Then he announces the *number* of his bid, but not the suit.

If he does not want to bid, he says, "I pass."

Blanca, on his left, then bids higher than Peter (if he has bid), or she passes. Doris then bids or passes. Each bid made must be higher than the one preceding it, and no one must name the suit, only the number. Ronald then bids or passes—and the bidding ends.

(If all four pass, the cards must be shuffled and dealt again by the same dealer—but this rarely happens.)

The player who has made the highest bid now names the trump suit. Suppose Peter has said, "Seven," Blanca, "Nine," Doris, "Ten." Ronald, "Pass." Doris, the highest bidder, now says, "Ten Spades."

Each player was dealt nine cards, but he must have only six when the play begins. He must discard at least three, and he may discard as many more as he pleases—all nine if he wants to—laying the discards face-up on the table.

(It is best to discard everything but trumps—and do not forget that the Five of the same color, *Left Pedro*, is a trump. Even an Ace of another suit is of no value, for it will not win any of the cards—all of them trumps —that count points.)

When everyone has discarded, Ronald takes up the pack which he placed face-down and, beginning with Peter, deals Peter, then Blanca, then Doris each enough cards to bring his or her hand up to six (if Peter discarded five of his nine cards, he will now need two more to make six; if Doris discarded all nine, she will need six new cards).

Ronald, instead of dealing himself the number of cards he needs, *robs the deck*. He looks at all the cards that remain in the deck and picks out from them as many as he needs to fill his hand, to bring it up to six. If there are any trumps that Ronald does not want (because he has six) he puts them face-up on the table among the discards, where all may see them.

If there should not be enough cards remaining in the deck to bring Ronald's hand up to six, he must take some of the discards.

The player who was the highest bidder and has named the trump suit leads for the first trick.

Everyone must follow suit or trump. He does not have to follow suit if he prefers to trump. If trump is led, and the *Left Pedro* is the only trump held, it must be played, of course. (For example, if Spades are trump, Doris leads a Spade, Blanca has no Spade, but has the ♣5, she must play it, because it is a trump.)

The highest card of the suit led wins the trick, unless a trump has been played on it. The trumps rank in this order:

A-K-Q-J-10-9-8-7-6-5 (*Right Pedro*), 5 of the same color (*Left Pedro*), 4-3-2.

If a player fails to follow suit or trump, when he can do so, his side may not score any points at all for that deal, the other side scoring only the number of points it has won.

The winner of each trick leads for the next trick.

When all six tricks have been played, each side counts the points it has won: *High*, 1; *Low*, 1; *Jack*, 1; *Game* (the Ten of trumps only), 1; *Right Pedro*, 5; *Left Pedro*, 5.

If Peter named the trump suit, having bid 9, and his side now has a total of 11 points, Peter and Doris score 11; and Ronald and Blanca score 3, the points they have won.

If, however, Peter bid 9 and made only 8, he has failed to make his bid. His side scores nothing, and Ronald and Blanca score the 6 points they made, plus the 1 point Peter failed to win to make his bid; so the score would be: Peter's side, 0; Ronald's side, 7.

The deal passes each time to the left. This gives everyone, in turn, the privilege of "robbing the deck."

The first side to reach 51 points wins the game.

49. Cooncan

Cooncan is based on an old Spanish game, but just why it should have been called *Con quién?* (With whom?) nobody seems to know. It is a favorite game for two players, especially in the South and Southwest.

Only forty cards are used. All the Tens, Nines, and Eights are removed from the pack. The object is to be the first to lay eleven cards face-up on the table.

The cards may be laid on the table only when they are *triplets* (three of a kind, such as three Jacks), *fours* (four of a kind, as four Sevens), or *sequences*—three or more cards of the same suit that follow in regular order, as:

A sequence may not have less than three cards, and the Ace may be used in sequence only before the 2, and never after the King (A-2-3, but not Q-K-A nor K-A-2).

Suppose that Craig and Betty are playing Cooncan, and Craig is the dealer. He shuffles the forty-card pack, and deals ten cards to each player, two at a time;

then he places the remainder of the pack on the table, face-down.

Both players sort their hands into *possible* triplets (two cards of a kind that may become a triplet when another card is drawn) and possible sequences. But they do not yet lay on the table any triplet, four, or sequence they may already hold.

Craig has dealt, so Betty has the first turn to play. She draws the top card from the stack, and places it face-up on the table in front of her. She must *never* take into her hand any card drawn from the stack.

If she can use the card she has drawn (to form a sequence, a triplet, or four) she lays face-up beside it the cards from her hand that form the combination with this card. She may lay down also any one or more combinations that she holds in her hand (any triplet, four, or sequence that was dealt to her).

A combination held in the hand when the cards are dealt may be placed on the table at any time that a card is used to form a combination. You may lay down as many combinations at one time as you choose.

If Betty does use the card she drew, it means that she now has eleven cards—on the table and in her hand. She may never have more than ten, so she must discard one from her hand—any card she thinks she will not need. She places it face-up in front of Craig. And then it is his turn to play.

If Betty cannot use the card she drew from the pack and placed in front of her, she pushes it across the table to Craig, and it lies face-up in front of him. And it is his turn to play. She will not have to discard from her hand, because she has discarded the card she drew.

Craig may use the card Betty has given him—to form a triplet, four, or sequence. If he does use it, he may lay down also any combination that was dealt to him, and then he must discard, placing his discard face-up in front of Betty.

If he does not want the card Betty gave him, he lays it aside, face-down, and it is out of the game. He then draws the top card off the pack and places it face-up in front of him—to use if he wants it, discarding some card (placing the discard in front of Betty) if he uses it. Or if he does not want the card he drew, he slides it across the table to Betty.

Betty then either uses the card Craig has given her and discards (giving him her discard) or casts it aside, out of the game, draws the next top card, and then discards (either the card she drew or, if she uses it, one from her hand).

Always when a card is used, the player must discard one card to keep his hand (including the cards on the table) to ten cards. And always the last one to refuse to use a card—the one who casts it aside, out of the game—is the one who draws the next card from the face-down pack.

In this way the entire pack is gone through, each one playing in turn—drawing a card, laying down cards, then discarding.

A triplet that has been laid down may be increased to four at any time. If Betty has three Queens down, and later gets another, by drawing it or by Craig's discard, she may place it beside the three and thus have four cards on the table—four of the eleven she wants to get down to win the game.

In the same way a sequence may be increased at either end by adding one card at a time. If Betty has on the table:

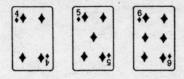

she may add the ◊7, then the ◊J, then Queen, then King, or at the other end the ◊3, then 2, then Ace.

A set of four may be decreased to a triplet. If Craig has on the table:

and holds the ♣A and draws the ♣3, he may lay down his A and 3 by "borrowing" one of the 2's; so he will then have on the table:

    ♠2   ♡2   ◊2 and ♣A ♣2 ♣3

In the same way a player may form a triplet by "borrowing" from either end of a sequence *that has more than three cards.* If Craig has on the table:

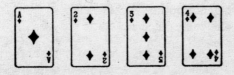

he may borrow either the Ace or the 4, by laying down
two more to complete the triplet. If he borrows the
Ace, he will have:

$$\diamond A \qquad \spadesuit A \qquad \clubsuit A \quad \text{and} \quad \diamond 2 \qquad \diamond 3 \qquad \diamond 4$$

Three cards must always be left in a sequence.

A player will usually *want* to use a card when he
can, but he does not *have* to do so unless the other
player "forces" him.

Suppose Craig has a sequence of 6-7-J on the table
and draws a Queen, but does not want to use it, because he is planning another way to get eleven cards
down for game. He discards the Queen he has drawn,
by shoving it across the table to Betty. She may, if she
thinks she can block his plans, force him to use it, by
placing the card at the end of his sequence, and saying, "Discard." In that case he must discard some card
from his hand.

In the same way she can force him to use one of her
discards (to add to a triplet he has in front of him, or
at one end of a sequence) by placing the card in position quickly and saying, "Discard," before he can cast
it aside, face-down, out of the game.

When a player is out of cards—all ten lying on the
table—he continues to draw from the pack in alternate
turns, and to watch the opponent's discard for the one
card he needs to complete his eleven (the end card of
a sequence, or the fourth to a triplet).

The player who first has eleven cards on the table
wins the game.

If neither player has eleven cards down when the
last card has been drawn from the pack and used or
passed, the game is a tie, neither one winning.

50. Five Hundred

This is an interesting game for three players, and an even better game for four, playing partners.

The full pack and the Joker are used. If there is a trump suit, the Joker becomes the highest trump. If the game is played at No Trump, the Joker is a lone trump all by itself.

Three cards are dealt to each player, then three to the "Widow," face down in the center of the table. Then two more to each player, then three more, then two more. This will give each one ten cards, and there will be three in the Widow. The remainder of the pack is laid aside, face-down, not to be used in the game.

The object is to win 500 points—by bidding and taking a certain number of *tricks*. The trick values are:

No. of Tricks	6	7	8	9	10
Spades	40	140	240	340	440
Clubs	60	160	260	360	460
Diamonds	80	180	280	380	480
Hearts	100	200	300	400	500
No Trump	120	220	320	420	520

No one may bid less than 6 tricks (agreeing to take six out of a total of ten tricks), and he must name the suit as well as the number—"6 Hearts," "7 Spades," "8 No Trump."

The bidding is begun by the player on the dealer's left, and each one in turn has a chance to bid or pass. There is only one round of bidding. Should everyone at the table pass, the cards are gathered up, shuffled, and dealt by the next player on the left.

Each bid must be higher in *value* than the bid preceding it. (6 Diamonds, worth 80, is higher than 6

Clubs, worth 60. 7 Clubs is higher than 7 Spades.)

Suppose Dion and Garnet are playing partners against Kent and Jane.

Jane begins the bidding with 7 No Trump. If Garnet, next, wants to bid Clubs she must say 8 Clubs, for 7 Clubs (worth 160) would not be higher than 7 No Trump (worth 220).

If Garnet says 8 Clubs, Kent, next, may say 8 Hearts, if he wants to, for that is higher than 8 Clubs.

Dion, the dealer, may then bid still higher, or he may pass. (The bidding will not be confusing if you keep the table of trick values in front of you until the bidding is finished.)

The player who wins the bid, by being the highest bidder, *scores only the value of the tricks bid,* unless he wins *every* trick. In that case, he scores 250 if the value of his bid was less than 250.

(For example, if Dion bids 6 Clubs and wins 9 tricks, he scores for only 6 Clubs, 60; but if he bids 6 Clubs and wins all 10 tricks, he scores 250. If he bids 8 Hearts and wins all 10 tricks, he scores only the 300 his 8 Hearts are worth.)

When the bidding is finished (everyone having bid or passed), the highest bidder picks up the three cards in the Widow, adds them to his hand, and discards any three he pleases, laying them aside face-down, out of the game. He then leads for the first trick.

Everyone must follow suit if he can. He may not play the Joker, which is a trump, if he can follow suit. If he cannot follow suit, he may play either a trump or another suit.

The highest card of the suit led wins the trick, unless it is trumped. If a trump is led and the Joker is played, it wins the trick, being the highest trump.

If the game is being played at No Trump, the one who holds the Joker must follow suit if he can, but if he has no card of the suit led, he may play the Joker as a lone trump, and it will take the trick.

If at No Trump someone leads the Joker, he must say what suit he wants it to be, such as "Hearts"—and everyone must play that suit if he can. The Joker takes the trick, being higher than the Ace of the suit named.

The winner of each trick leads for the next one.

Every trick taken in must be neatly stacked face-down, overlapping, but not covering, the one below it. These tricks may not be inspected again during the play.

When the ten tricks have been played, the bidder is the first to mark down his score (if two are playing partners, their scores are counted together, of course). The other players then score 10 points for each trick they have captured. (If Kent and Jane won the seven tricks Kent bid in Hearts, they score 200, and Dion and Garnet score 30—10 points for each of the three tricks they won. If Kent and Jane won nine tricks, they would still score only 200—the value of the seven tricks bid—and Dion and Garnet would score 10, for the one trick they took.)

If the bidder fails to take as many tricks as he bid, he is "set back" (has deducted from his score) 100 points for each trick he lacks. (If Kent bids 8 Hearts, and he and Jane take only 6 tricks, they have 200 deducted from their score—100 for each of the two tricks they lack; while Dion and Garnet score 40 for the four tricks they take.) The side that first reaches 500 points wins the game.

AN EASY LESSON IN
CONTRACT BRIDGE

Children often become discouraged when they try
to learn Contract, because it seems difficult and confusing. That is because they jump into the middle of
it without first learning the beginning. A well-built
house must have a solid foundation!

*The game given here will prove the foundation for
later good playing.*

The First Step

The first step is to learn something about the game
and to become familiar with Contract "language."

Contract Bridge is a game for four, playing partners. The pack of fifty-two cards is used. This gives
each of the four players thirteen cards, and makes
thirteen tricks when all the cards have been played.

Contract is a bidding game. You "contract" to take

so many tricks *more than six*. If you think you and your partner can take seven of the total thirteen tricks, you bid, not seven, but *one*—one more than six. If you think you can take eight tricks, you bid *two*, if nine, *three*, and so on.

If you take twelve tricks out of the total thirteen, that is a *Small Slam*. If you take all thirteen tricks, it is a *Grand Slam*.

A *Rubber* is two games won out of three. If one side wins the first two games, that completes the Rubber, and the third game is not played, but a new Rubber is begun.

A side is *Vulnerable* when it has won one game of a Rubber. It is *Not Vulnerable* when it has not yet won a game.

The suits rank in value in this order, with No Trump the highest and Clubs the lowest: *No Trump, Spades, Hearts, Diamonds, Clubs.*

Spades and Hearts are the *Major suits*. Diamonds and Clubs are the *Minor suits*.

Honors are the Ace, King, Queen, Jack and Ten of a suit.

About Scoring

A game is 100 points.

Each trick is worth so many points that count toward game. But you may *score only the number of tricks you bid*. (If you bid Two Hearts, and take all thirteen tricks, you score toward game only the two you bid. You do get credit in the "honor score" for the other five tricks—called "overtricks," tricks won over the number you bid—but only those you bid score toward *game*.)

That is why Contract bidding is important. You want to bid as high as you safely can, so you can score as much as possible. Yet you must not bid too high, because if you fail, you score nothing, and the other side scores.

And that is why Contract is a team-work game. You and your partner must understand each other's bid, so you can reach a suit (or No Trump) that will fit both your hands.

The *value of the tricks bid and won* is scored toward game *below* the line on the score-pad. All other values are marked in the "honor score" above the line.

Doubling multiplies all trick values by 2; and *redoubling* multiplies them by 4. (Two Hearts, for example, would score 60; if doubled, 120; if redoubled, 240.)

A scoring table is given on the last page, for you to refer to, but it will be much easier for you to get some grown-up to show you how to score.

Dealing

First of all, you draw cards to see who will be partners and who will deal. (After the first hand, the deal passes each time to the next one on the left of the last dealer.) The pack is spread face-down on the table, and everyone draws a card. The two with the highest cards are partners. And the one with the highest card of all deals. (Ace is higher than King.) If there is a tie, the cards rank in this order: Spades, Hearts, Diamonds, Clubs.

Suppose the four players are Ann and Bob playing against Carol and Denis. And Ann is the dealer.

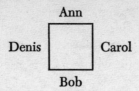

Carol shuffles the cards, and Denis cuts them by lifting the top part and placing it toward Ann. Ann puts the bottom part on the top and deals the cards around, one at a time, beginning with Carol.

No one must touch a card until Ann has dealt the last one to herself. Then everyone picks up his hand and sorts the cards into suits. (It is usual to arrange them Spades, Hearts, Clubs, Diamonds, thus separating the colors—even though in bidding their rank is Spades, Hearts, Diamonds, Clubs.)

The dealer has the first bid, then each in turn to the left round and round the table, until after some bid the three other players all pass. (If all four pass on the first round, the hand is not played, and there must be a new deal by the next player on the left.)

Valuing Your Hand

Ann, as dealer, must bid or pass. But how shall she know which to do? She must first "value" her hand, decide what it is worth—whether, with her partner's help, she can probably take at least seven (*one* more than six) of the thirteen tricks. If she believes she can take seven or more tricks with Hearts trump, she bids *One Heart.*

(Grown-ups sometimes begin by bidding Two or more; but it will be easier, while you are learning, to begin always with One.)

In valuing her hand, Ann looks first at the high cards in it. And she must know how much those high cards are worth, for unless she holds a "count" of at least 2½ she must not bid One, but must pass. She can count 1 for each Ace she holds, for it will probably take 1 trick, 2 if she holds the Ace-King together, and so on.

The counting values of the high cards (given here in table form) should be learned very thoroughly, for until you are able to value your hand you cannot bid correctly.

(*x*, in the table, means any card lower than 10. Cards listed together, as K-Q, must be in the same suit.)

A-K	..2	A K-Q K-J-x	..1
A-J-10 A-Q K-Q-J K-Q-10	..1½	K-x Q-J-x	..½

A-K always counts 2, no matter how many cards are with it, such as A-K-Q or A-K-Q-J. Of course, if that suit should be trump, A-K-Q-J would take 4 tricks, but at the time you are valuing your hand you do not know which suit will be trump, so you can count only 2 tricks.

A-Q always counts 1½, even if it should be A-Q-J or A-Q-10.

A-J counts only 1 (for the Ace), but with a 10 also, it becomes more valuable, so *A-J-10* counts 1½.

K-Q counts 1, but with a J or 10 added, it is more valuable, so *K-Q-J or K-Q-10* counts 1½.

Suppose you held:

♠A-K-Q-9-7   ♡J-10-4   ◇J-6   ♣K-J-9

you would count 2 in Spades (A-K) and 1 in Clubs (K-J-x), a total count of 3.

Or if you held:

♠A-Q-J-4   ♡Q-J-10   ◇A-J-8   ♣K-Q-10

you would count 1½ in Spades (A-Q-J); ½ in Hearts (Q-J-10); 1 in Diamonds (A); 1½ in Clubs (K-Q-10) —a total of 4½.

Deal out a few hands and value them with the table of values beside you—until you can do so without having to refer to the table.

Can you value these hands:

(1) ♠A-K-9-8-6   ♡J-8-7-3   ◇A-9-5   ♣K
(2) ♠K-Q-5   ♡Q-6-2   ◇A-K-Q-J-3   ♣A-K
(3) ♠A-5   ♡Q-J-9-7   ◇A-J-10-9-4   ♣K-6
(4) ♠K-Q-J-10   ♡A-Q-7-3   ◇K   ♣K-J-6-2
(5) ♠A-K-J-3-2   ♡6-4   ◇K-Q-10-9   ♣K-Q

(The answers are in a footnote on page 120.)

Bidding

The bidding, beginning with the dealer, is always in turn to the left; and ends only when three players in succession have passed.

In bidding, you say both the *number* of tricks you "contract" to take and the *suit* (or No Trump)—such as "One Spade," "One No Trump," "Two Clubs."

Every bid must be higher—either in the *rank of the suit* (Clubs, Diamonds, Hearts, Spades, No Trump) or in the *number of tricks*—than the bid that precedes it.

(If you bid One Heart, the next player may bid One

Spade or One No Trump, because they are higher in *rank* than Hearts; but if he wants to bid Diamonds or Clubs, he must say Two, a higher *number* of tricks.)

The first one to bid is called the "Opening Bidder," or sometimes the "Original Bidder." (If Ann bids, she is the Opening Bidder. If she passes and Carol bids, Carol is the Opening Bidder.)

To bid One in any suit the Opening Bidder must have a count in high cards of at least 2½. If the count is less than 2½ she should pass.

This refers to the Dealer (Ann), and Second Hand (Carol). If the Third Hand or Fourth Hand (Bob or Denis) should be the Opening Bidder, he must have a high-card count of at least 3, because his partner has passed, showing weakness in high cards.

But to bid One, there is another requirement that is just as important as the high-card count. That is the *length* of the suit—the number of cards in it.

Never bid a suit that has less than four cards. And you must have a count of at least 1½ *in a four-card* suit, to bid it, and a count of at least ½ *in a five-card* suit. (This is not in addition to, but part of, the 2½ high-card count in the entire hand.)

Suppose Ann holds:

♠6-5-3-2   ♡A-K-2   ◇9-8-6   ♣A-K-5

she should pass on the first round of bidding, even though she has a total high-card count of 4. Her only suit *long* enough to bid (four cards) does not have 1½ high-card count in it; therefore she should not bid it.

Answers to Hands on page 119: (1) 3; (2) 5; (3) 3½; (4) 4; (5) 4½

If she holds:

♠ K-10-8-5-3   ♡ A-K-Q   ◊ 9-8   ♣ Q-J-5

she should bid "One Spade," for in a *five*-card suit she requires only a count of ½, and she has ½ in Spades and a total of 3 in her hand.

Suppose you hold *two* four-card suits, or two five-card suits, or one five-card and one four-card, and each of them has enough high cards to make it biddable. Which shall you bid first?

If two biddable suits are the same length—two four-cards or two five-cards—*bid the higher ranking one first,* remembering that the suits rank in this order: Spades, Hearts, Diamonds, Clubs.

Bid One Spade:
    ♠ K-Q-8-7-5   ♡ A-K-9-6-4   ◊ 8-6   ♣ 7
Bid One Diamond:
    ♠ A-4   ♡ 10-7-2   ◊ A-Q-J-5   ♣ A-Q-J-9
Bid One Heart:
    ♠ 3   ♡ A-J-10-5-3   ◊ J-9   ♣ A-K-6-3-2
Bid One Heart:
    ♠ 7-6-3-2   ♡ A-J-10-5   ◊ A-K-J-6   ♣ K

(Spades are higher ranking than Hearts, but a four-card suit without 1½ high-card count is not biddable.)

If two biddable suits are of different length—one five-card and one four-card—*bid the longer one first.*

Bid One Heart:
    ♠ A-K-Q-5   ♡ K-Q-9-5-3   ◊ 8-4   ♣ J-2
Bid One Diamond:
    ♠ A-Q-J-10   ♡ 9-4   ◊ K-J-7-5-3   ♣ 6-2
Bid One Heart:
    ♠ K   ♡ A-Q-9-8-2   ◊ K-J-9   ♣ A-K-10-7
Bid One Club:
    ♠ K-Q-10-7   ♡ A-J-3   ◊ 3   ♣ K-J-9-6-5

What should you bid, if you were the Opening Bidder, and held these cards? (Remember the rule: If two suits are of *equal* length, bid the *higher ranking*. If of *unequal* length, bid the *longer*.)

(1) ♠K-Q-10-6-5 ♡A-Q-10-6-5 ◇J ♣7-6
(2) ♠6-4 ♡10 ◇A-K-9-7-3 ♣A-J-9-7-3
(3) ♠7-6-5-3 ♡A-Q-10-4 ◇A-K-9-5 ♣8
(4) ♠A-K-7-6-3 ♡K-Q-10-9-4-2 ◇3 ♣J
(5) ♠A-K-10-9 ♡7-3 ◇K-Q-9-7-5 ♣8-6

(The answers are in a footnote on page 123.)

If you are the Opening Bidder, *never bid One No Trump if you can bid a suit.*

Bid One No Trump if you have no biddable suit, but do have a count of at least 3 plus ("plus" means two or more Tens or Jacks or Queens in addition to the count of 3) *and your high cards are in at least three suits.*

Suppose you held:

♠A-K-5   ♡A-10-4   ◇K-Q-7   ♣10-6-5-2

No suit would be *long* enough (four cards) to bid except Clubs, and it is not *strong enough* (it lacks 1½ count). While you could not bid any suit, with this hand, neither must you pass, with your total count of 4, or you might deceive your partner into believing that you have a worthless hand. So your bid would be One No Trump.

When you bid One in a suit (One Spade, One Heart, One Diamond, or One Club) for the Opening Bid, you say to your partner (not out loud, of course! But it is what your bid means to him): "I have a high-card count of not less than 2½—I may have more than that, but you can count on me for 2½ anyway. I have at least four cards in the suit I bid, and a count of at least $1\frac{1}{2}$ in it, if it is of four cards, and at least $\frac{1}{2}$ if it is of five or more cards."

When you bid One No Trump, it is the same as if you said aloud to him: "Partner, I do not have any biddable suit, but I do have a count of at least 3 plus in high cards; and my high cards are not bunched together in one suit, nor two, but are in at least three suits."

When you pass it tells him that you have no biddable suit, and not enough high cards (distributed in three suits) to bid No Trump.

This bidding information, for the *Opening Bidder*, is so important for you to know, that it is best to repeat it in a little table:

A suit to be biddable must have four or more cards. If it has four cards, it must have a high-card count of at least $1\frac{1}{2}$, and if five cards, at least $\frac{1}{2}$ high-card count.

When two biddable suits are of equal length, bid the higher ranking one first.

When two biddable suits are of unequal length, bid the longer one first.

To bid One in a suit, Dealer or Second Hand must hold a total high-card count of at least $2\frac{1}{2}$. Third or Fourth Hand must have at least 3.

To bid One No Trump, any player must have a high-card count of at least 3 plus. And the high cards must be distributed in at least three suits.

Do not bid No Trump if you can bid a suit.

Now to go back to the game that Ann and Bob are playing against Carol and Denis.

Suppose Ann has dealt these cards to the four players:

Answers to Hands on page 122: (1) One Spade, (2) One Diamond, (3) One Heart, (4) One Heart, (5) One Diamond.

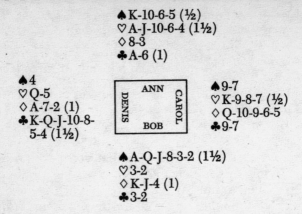

Ann, being the dealer, has the first bid. She sees that her hand has a high-card count of 3, and that she has only one biddable suit for an Opening Bid.

(The Spade suit is *long* enough, but not strong enough, having only ½ instead of 1½ required for a four-card suit.) Even if the Spades were strong enough, Ann would still bid Hearts, for she remembers the rule:

When two biddable suits are of unequal length, bid the longer one first.

So Ann says, "One Heart."

Carol holds a high-card count of only ½, and she knows that to make a Defensive Bid (a bid after Ann has opened the bidding) she must have at least 1½. Even her five Diamonds are too weak to bid, with not enough high cards in other suits to help them—and of course she would have to say Two Diamonds, to be higher than One Heart. Carol can only say, "Pass."

Bob, as partner of the Opening Bidder, must do one of three things: *Raise*, by bidding higher in his partner's suit; *Takeout*, by bidding higher in another suit (or No Trump); or *Pass*.

To raise (her bid of One Heart to Two Hearts) he must hold *four small cards* in her suit, or *three if one is an Ace, King, or Queen*. This is called "Normal Trump Support."

Bob does not have Normal Trump Support, so he cannot raise Ann's Heart bid. But he can easily takeout by bidding Spades. That will say to Ann: "I may or may not have Normal Trump Support, but I want to tell you that I have Spades, so that we can fit our hands together, with the suit that is best for both of us."

Bob bids, "One Spade."

Denis, even though his partner passed (showing a weak hand), counts seven tricks that he is sure of taking alone with Clubs trump (six in Clubs and one in Diamonds), and surely with his partner's help he can manage one more. So Denis bids, "Two Clubs."

Ann looks at her hand. Her partner Bob has told her by his bid that he has a good Spade hand, so she must tell him that she can help him very nicely in Spades. Then if he holds good Hearts and wants to switch back to her suit, all well and good.

So Ann says, "Two Spades."

Carol has no help for Denis in Clubs, and nothing else strong enough to bid; so again she says, "Pass."

Bob, knowing now that Ann has both Hearts and Spades, is a little afraid to jump to Four Spades (which would be a game), because his hand and Ann's together might not be worth that. So Bob says, "Three Spades."

Denis passes.

Ann has a good helping hand for her partner's suit,

and she believes that together they can take ten tricks, so she bids for game: "Four Spades."

Carol passes.

Bob passes.

Denis passes.

And so the bidding ends, and Bob (because it was he and not Ann who first said Spades) must play the hand at Four Spades. Bob is called the *Declarer*—the one who "declared" the trump.

In table form the bidding would look like this:

	Ann	Carol	Bob	Denis
1st round:	1 Heart	Pass	1 Spade	2 Clubs
2nd round:	2 Spades	Pass	3 Spades	Pass
3rd round:	4 Spades	Pass	Pass	Pass

Playing

With the bidding completed, they are ready to play the hand—with Spades for trump.

The player on the Declarer's left always leads for the first trick. Denis leads the King of Clubs.

After he has led, Ann lays her hand on the table, face-up, and she takes no further part in the game. She is the *Dummy*—the partner of the Declarer. Bob will play her hand as well as his own.

Bob plays the ♣A from Dummy on Denis's ♣K. Carol plays the ♣9. Then Bob plays from his own hand the ♣2; and wins the trick with Dummy's Ace.

Every player *must follow suit* if he can. If he cannot follow suit, he may play either a trump or a card of another suit, as he chooses. The highest card of the suit led wins the trick, unless it has been trumped.

The winner of each trick leads for the next one. If a card from Dummy wins the trick, a card must be led from Dummy.